This Too Shall Pass

Written by Neesha Duncan

For ordering information, permission, or questions contact:
Neeshaduncan@gmail.com

https://www.amazon.com

Edited by Jennifer Dryden & Diana K Dungy
Cover by Alison Ruble & Emmanuel Hollins

Note from my Therapist

Trauma is a term that has been widely used within recent years. It has been used to define hardships endured by individuals. As a graduate student at Drake University in Des Moines, IA

I learned a new definition from Andrew Jacobs: 'something that happened to someone, that they didn't ask for and they are left alone to figure it out'. These acts could include anything from sexual abuse, physical abuse, emotional neglect, to losing a loved one or being in a car accident.

In 2015, the national average for children experiencing trauma was 683,000*. This could be a child at your church, your local grocery store, or at your neighborhood school. The signs of abuse vary for each child, but what remains true for all the children is their feeling of fear.

Learning how to disguise the pain of mental, sexual, and physical abuse becomes a hard task. Problems focusing during academic classes, feeling disconnected from others, and not understanding how to use their voice becomes a daily annoyance.

To exert this stress, youth may get into toxic relationships with their peers (friends and romantic partners), use anger in unhealthy ways, and isolate to avoid further maltreatment.

If left unaddressed, the youth will grow up unhealed and with the potential of being out of control: of their emotions, health, and behavior.

The author of this book took a risk to improve her holistic wellness by breaking her code of silence. She chose her life and her voice to dispel the lies that kept her stuck in her pain. In this book you will find pure humanity being defiled by family and acquaintances.

She will share her experiences that stunted, confused, angered, and eventually freed her.

You will find intersectionality in various forms, as well as, as moments of resilience. Please use your heart when reading this book and take time to reflect on areas of your life that may require healing.

Breanne Ward, CRC, LMHC
ForWard Consulting, LLC

TABLE OF CONTENTS

TABLE OF CONTENTS (CONTINUED)

Introduction

Most who suffer a trauma feel as though they have to suffer in silence. They feel alone and ashamed, as if no one will listen or understand. They fear others may just view them as whiny, looking for a pity party, or perhaps even a liar.

I am very familiar with this and wanted to share my story in hopes of reaching those like me who have or are currently going through situations of trauma. My decision to share my story does not come from a place of anger or spite. Pull on your strengths and don't let it suffocate you.

Whether it be a situation just like mine, similar or even worse, you are not alone. You can survive, heal and even thrive.

I'd like to share my journey of confusion, sadness, hurt, pain, anger, forgiveness and healing. Share how my trauma affected me in ways people may not realize, including small triggers.

In my writing, I speak to you as the child I was and share feelings I felt at that time.

Please forgive me for some of the language used, but I wanted to tell it as it was. I went through phases.

Going through my pain I would often tell myself This 'Too Shall Pass' and that's where the title came from.

For so long life was so heavy. I finally reached a point of loving myself.

I LOVE ME SOME ME!

'True story'

CHAPTER 1

Momma's Comin

Sometimes childhood can be so confusing. The weight put on us as a child when we're caught in the middle of our parents' differences, especially when they're no longer together.

Parents don't often think of the damages their choices or actions can do to their kids. We comprehend more than they think we do. They must forget that part of their childhood. We see, we may not fully understand, but we see what they're doing, and feel the pain of their actions.

We soak it up like little sponges. I'm a parent now and I know I've made some bad choices. Oh man. I often think to myself,

"What have I done to my kids?"

My earliest memory is of going from home to home as a child at four years old. My parents were divorced and fighting over me. I don't have any memories of them actually being together.

For a time, I stayed with my mom then daddy and back to mom and even with my youngest sister's grandma. I remember being at my mom's in a duplex across the street from a park.

The parades always go down our street, Forest Avenue. All the excitement and noise from the drums sometimes scares me. I run into the house screaming when I see the clowns coming, some walking tall on stilts.

Doing their tricks with balloons and flips. Throwing tootsie rolls our way. Kind of scary. Once they pass, I go back out to pick up what candy my sister's didn't get and watch the rest of the parade.

Fascinated by the horses all dressed up and prancing by. The clothes on the people riding the horses. I like to look at the horses, but I don't want to touch them. The older fancy cars honking their horns.

Enjoying the sounds of the loud drums, watching the drill teams marching by. They stop close by our house and we can watch them dance. Kids to adults high stepping. It's so much excitement.

Then at about the age of six or seven I go to my daddy's house and I'm a daddy's girl, his little princess. He always makes me feel special, like I'm his favorite. Always telling me how pretty I am, how my sisters are jealous of me and the way he treats me.

Most of the time I get whatever I want, and I don't want to share my daddy or my toys, so I get a little uncomfortable when my two younger sisters, by him, come over. It's an evil stare down whenever my daddy's not looking.

They have the same mom and most of the time I feel funny when they're around. I don't know why, I just do. Seems like we just can't get along at all.

Not even with the babysitter, Jan, who watches us at our house while my daddy's at work. She's so mean, ugly and a horrible cook. Making us noodles with no seasoning. No flavor at all. I add ketchup to force it down, but when my daddy walks in I can throw it away and ask for something else.

I don't think she likes us. *Why say you're going to watch kids you don't even like just to be mean to them?*

Sometimes she stays a little while after my dad gets home from work. I don't like having her here.

My younger sister, Natalie, and I give each other dirty looks all the time for no reason. We can't play together. I don't know why we don't get along.

Our other sister is eleven months older than Natalie and quiet. Even though I never really played with her either, I feel bad when she passes away from cancer at the age of three.

I wish I had a better relationship with her now that she's gone. *Why was I so mean?* Makes me feel like a horrible sister and It's too late.

My daddy keeps a musical jewelry box with some of her things in it. The thing that sticks with me the most is a ball of her soft, curly, dark brown hair.

She had a cute little soft face and always sad, sad from the pain, I guess. I can still see her face with her teary eyes. That's the only face I can remember. Not a smile or even peaceful face. I really wish I was nicer to her. I wish I had better memories with her.

I don't even know why I was so mean, and I doubt she felt the same way about me. How could she? She was probably in too pain from her sickness to be worried about me. Maybe the anger came from having different moms.

We don't come from the same mom so I don't like you, or maybe this is my daddy and I don't want to share him with you.

Who knows?

Living in different homes and our mom's not liking each other, 'cause they don't. They don't get along either.

I just know we don't play well together at all and I feel uncomfortable at home. I try to avoid being in the same room or being alone with Natalie and I hate feeling or thinking this way. At bedtime, I want to fall asleep quick.

Jan takes us for a walk one day while my daddy's at work. Her and my sisters are walking ahead of me. It's so hot and the sun is beaming down on my face.

We just make it around the corner and up the block a little way when I see my mom's little head over the steering wheel driving down the street in this long, light blue, two-door car with the windows down.

I don't know the name of it, but she stops as soon as she sees me, leans over to open the passenger door, and tells me to get in.

Jan doesn't say a word. She looks at me and I look at her.

Then my mom yells at me to hurry up and get in the car, so I do. As soon as I get in and close the door we drive off.

She doesn't like Jan either and drives off cursing and yelling about my daddy and that bitch, Jan. I don't know what's going on, but my mom is very upset.

She's taking me home with her, which isn't a long drive from my daddy's house, and I know from all the yelling and cursing that she's not gonna let my daddy come and get me for a while.

CHAPTER 2
Mommy Dearest

My mom takes me home to my other three sisters and a couple of Doberman pinschers. I'm the third child in line. She tied her tubes after having my younger sister, Penny, who's two years behind me.

Ruby is the oldest, five years over me and Connie is two years over me. We live in a three-bedroom ranch style home on a dead-end street with the woods directly to the right of us.

There's a green apple tree in the front yard and a couple blackberry trees on the other side of the driveway to the left. They taste good, but stain everything.

We get a bowl from the kitchen to pick them. Rinse them in water and put a little salt on them. Laundry poles to the left of the yard as well where my mom hangs our sheets and some of our clothes.

The neighbor across the street hates us half the time. One day she's yelling at us, telling us to go back to Africa where we belong. The next day she's inviting us over for treats. Other days she yells at us to stay away from her yard.

We're at the end of a dead-end street, so we play in the street a lot. Her hedges are so high we can't see over them and they span her entire yard with an opening for the driveway.

She leaves her yard to come out in the street and yell at us. We just laugh at her cause she's crazy!

We like going into the woods to play. There's a shallow creek with frogs and garter snakes. We catch a snake one day, take it home, and tie a string around its neck to hang it from the laundry pole in the yard.

Then we throw rocks at it until it stops moving, take it down and cut it open down the middle to see the inside.

Ruby always has my sisters and I doing crazy things. That's big sis, what can we say? Mom always leaves us alone and she's the oldest and makes sure we know it.

With four girls we have a lot of "hand me downs." The clothes we hang onto way too long, but thank God for leg warmers. They come in real handy with those high waters.

When mom is rushing us out of the house, we have to throw on something quick and go. Sometimes it's the highwaters.

For the most part, we have plenty of clothes. My mom wants to make sure we look good in public. She says that's why she's always working so she can buy us things.

My little fur coat is one of my favorites and when I wear it you can't tell me nothin'! I'm too cute in my coat that looks like raccoon fur. It's mine baby!

Riding bikes is another thing we enjoy and I'm going so fast down the hill one day that I can't stop before hitting a parked car. My front tire goes under the car and I fall kind of hard.

I look up to a bunch of kids in a yard laughing at me. Stupid dummies! The worst part is struggling to pull the bike from under the car with them watching.

I couldn't just leave it. I thought about it. Now I'm walking back home with the bent tire that of course won't roll smoothly.

Having to walk the bike all the way back up the hill while they watched and laughed was so embarrassing. Talk about a walk of shame.

I didn't learn a lesson from it though. I go get on another bike with Ruby and Penny. Ruby on the seat, Penny on the pegs and me on the handlebars riding down a steep, sandy hill along the edge of the woods.

A truck drives by kind of fast leaking water from the back. He makes a sudden right turn cutting us off. Ruby has to hit the brakes really quick and the bike goes left towards the woods and a curb, sending us all flying.

All three of us got dusted and now we have permanent scars on our arms from that ride.

Being without mom so much we must do something to occupy ourselves. Especially in the summer. We start acting up a little bit. *She ain't around to see it, so it's alright.*

At this time, I'm about eight years old. We run up the block on the next street over checking for cars that have their windows down or doors unlocked. Looking for change in the ashtrays, maybe even taking a cassette tape. The change is to buy candy.

When we don't have money, we use our backpacks to steal candy on the way to school in the mornings. We get caught by security one morning.

I'm with Penny and a couple friends, but of course it's me that security catches stealing a candy bar, a Snicker's bar, my favorite.

We're taken to the back of the store, but he doesn't call the police nor our mom, instead he yells at us scaring us and kicks us out of the store. Tells us not to come back and we head off to school. I'm sad 'cause he kept my Snicker's bar.

Stupid!

After a while my mom's boyfriend, Anthony, moves in with us. Then she gets her tubes untied to have his baby. After this baby comes, making it five girls with me in the middle, mom moves us girls to the basement. All except the new baby, Layla.

It's not a nice finished basement. It's kind of like what you see in a scary movie, with a concrete wall on the left side of the stairs and it's open to the laundry room on the right side of the stairs.

As you get to the bottom of the stairs there's a room to the left with a few twin size beds and a wooden desk.

The floor is tiled with big black and white checkered squares in that room. Unfinished ceiling and no toilet.

There's a lot of fighting in the house. Anthony beats on my mom and us. Mom beats on us. Me and my sister's fight each other, except the youngest.

We love each other, but we're always fighting; hair pulling, stabbing, dragging each other down the stairs. I have to fight Connie and Penny on a regular basis. It seems like every day over the dumbest things.

It's like Penny picks at me on purpose. She likes to irritate me with a smile. She picks at me in the mornings while getting ready for school and it's way too early for this. She just keeps going until I can't take it anymore, so I grab her and start hitting her. Then it's Connie and I fighting.

It doesn't take much for her to come at me. She says I play too much. It doesn't have to be me bothering her directly. I can be doing something across the room that she doesn't like or look a certain way, that starts an argument and then a fight.

Feels like so much anger in the house. Fighting, fighting, fighting. Ruby and Connie fight each other a lot. Then they make me go out and fight for Penny.

She gets into it with somebody in the neighborhood because of her mouth and they come and get me to fight whoever she's arguing with. I don't get in fights in the neighborhood just because somebody has a problem with me.

Never!

Me and my sisters roam free, having fun with my mom being gone so much, but she's irritated with us when she gets home. She's out a lot between work and hanging out with her friends and boyfriend.

Sometimes we go to this daycare called, 'Tiny Tots' and other times we just stay home, except Layla. She's never left at home with the rest of us. She goes to her grandma on her dad's side.

The rest of us stay home and fend for ourselves while our mom is gone all day. She starts getting upset about all the food we eat while she's gone. Says we eat too much of her food, so she starts locking us in the basement while she's out and It feels like forever.

This is where we stay until she comes home and sometimes when she's home with company or Anthony just doesn't feel like looking at us.

Well, we get smart. We already know she's gonna lock us up again when she gets ready to leave, so we start sneaking food into the basement before lockdown.

We take whatever we can cook in our Easy Bake Oven. We pee in the basement drain, of course. Anthony comes down to the basement one night while we're sleeping and wakes us up yelling and beating us for pissing in the basement drain and having the basement smelling like piss.

My mom stands by while he beats us with two by four boards. The boards from the bottom of a box spring.

"What do they expect us to do down here? We can't hold it in all day? Come on now."

So angry with him, I go to school and show my teacher the bruises from the board, she tells me I "probably deserved it." She's kinda mean. I can't stand her. Her makeup looks like a clown, and she always calls me a bean pole 'cause I'm so skinny.

She's not gonna help and I'm sure nobody else will either. No point in telling anybody else. When Connie and Ruby go to school showing their bruises from the water hose and extension cord, they call the Department of Human Services.

They show up to the school and launch an investigation that doesn't go far because my mom says they did it to each other outside playing. They buy it or don't care and that's the end of that.

They treat us like dogs. He beats us and makes us clean it up. Every time! Hungry and tired of bein' beaten and having to clean our piss up, we have to find another way.

So, we figure out how to sneak upstairs while they're gone.

There's a hole in the floor of the bathroom linen closet that goes to the basement. It's a laundry shoot without the shoot.

Ruby and Connie push me up through the hole and I run around and unlock the basement door so we can eat, use the bathroom, and get a little fresh air. They all go back down after we eat and whatever else. I lock the basement door then jump down through the hole. Piece of cake!

Soon my mom realizes we're getting out of the basement by the evidence of disappearing food. She starts locking us outside. Now we have to stay in the backyard until she comes home.

Well now we have more space and fresh air, but still no food and can't figure out how to break into the house.

She takes me from my dad to bring me home to this and I don't understand why because it doesn't feel like she wants any of us except Layla. Still, I love her, and we'll play out here til she comes home to let us in.

We're not staying in this fenced in yard all day though. We will go play with friends and make it back to the yard before she gets home. If not, we know there will be a beatin.'

Anthony just enjoys beating us, punishing us. He enjoys it so much that he took it out on one of our dogs one night. He choked her to death right in front of us. Then they just laid a blanket over her in the yard. I don't know what they did with her after we went to bed.

Even though we're getting beat all the time by both of them I still feel sad for my mom when he turns on her. I don't like seeing her cry, so I yell at him, calling him stupid while Connie holds me back.

I get so mad. I want to beat him. I don't know what I can do with my little self, but I want to hurt him. I don't care if all I can do is scratch him up.

I want to protect her. She won't stand up for herself or us even though she has a gun in the house. I know she has the gun because she accidentally pulled it on Ruby one night for moving around the house in the middle of the night scaring her. She thought someone broke in. Guess she doesn't want to hurt him.

Well I do.

When I can catch a quiet moment, I'm glued to the TV. There's a band called KISS and the whole band has their faces painted. If they were standing right in front of me, I'd be so scared, but I know they're not coming through the screen.

Every time this band comes on TV I can't stop watching. I can't move until they leave the screen. I lay on the floor right in front of the TV not even paying attention to the music. I can't tell you what they sound like. Wouldn't know. It's the faces that have my attention. I pay no attention to anything else going on around me. I'm stuck until the video is over. Then I'm back to reality.

One night, my mom has us all lined up in the kitchen for questioning over the cornbread. She's so upset that somebody ate a piece of the cornbread. If we don't tell who ate the corn bread, we're all gonna get beat.

Now we all know who did it. It was Ruby and she done already told us we better not tell on her, so we can't. We're all in the kitchen scared and shaking 'cause she won't tell mom she ate the dang cornbread.

We're trying to hold in the tears, looking at this girl like, *"just tell her you ate it."*

She won't tell. She wants one of us to take the blame, so we all get beat over some funky cornbread.

If she doesn't want us to eat it, why in the hell did she make it? Is it just for looks??? Man!

We get in trouble for any and every lil thing. Oh please don't run in and out that dang door. Please don't.

"If you don't stop running in and out that damn door letting all the air out you gone getcho ass beat. Keep yo mutha fucken ass outside." "Why y'all got all these damn lights on? Y'all makin it hot in here. Turn the damn lights off."

Lady, if you don't hush!

Madness, madness. Penny loses her mind, I don't know why, but she takes a butter knife and tries to cut me over my eye. I remain calm and go to the kitchen to get me a knife, and not a butter knife.

I test it on a chair with that good ol thick floral plastic. I just wanna see how sharp it is first. It's good! Now I go and cut her upper arm. Just a little blood, but it's not bad.

Connie and Ruby come running to the rescue when Penny screams. They tell us to say she cut it on the desk, so I don't get beat. The corner of the desk is chipped. Cracked wood sticking out so my mom buys it. Saves me from a beatin.'

Then there's the miracle child, Layla. That's what me and my other sisters call her. She can do no wrong in our mom's eyes. She doesn't get beat, locked in the basement or outside the house cause that's her daddy's child.

Her grandma looks after her while my mom and Anthony are out doing whatever. She's the special one over here.

I take her out to play one day, being big sis and all. I put little sis in the stroller to take her on a short walk down the driveway while moms in the house. At nine years old I'm too young to take her too far.

I'm pushing her down the somewhat steep driveway in her stroller. I get to the end of the raggedy driveway and hit a little dip. Oops!

The stroller flips, she falls out and now she's crying.

Aw man!

I'm scared and panicking. I do not need my momma to hear her crying. I pick her up so fast dusting her big ass forehead off and lean in to tell her "Shut the hell up 'fore momma come out here, ain't nobody trynna get beat today."

I'm done playing with her.

She doesn't get the same treatment as the rest of us and at some point, my mom sends me to stay with her grandma for a bit. The grandma also keeps Anthony's sister's kids. There's five of them. The two oldest girls live here.

I sleep upstairs with them when I stay here. It's not as bad here. She's a good cook. Love her smothered pork chops. That's my favorite. My daddy comes to get me on weekends.

I have my strawberry shortcake collection over there that my daddy got me. I listen to The Jackson's and Diana Ross records with the oldest granddaughter. She's cool. I always feel comfortable around her.

I was okay with the second to the oldest. At least until she calls me into her room in the middle of a summer day.

She's a few years older than me. Her grandma is down in the kitchen nook where she spends a lot of time during the day.

She takes her shorts off and lays back against her pillow on her bed. She tells me to lick her between her legs. This is a game I don't want to play.

I don't like being dirty and putting my tongue on somebody's body part sounds dirty. I don't want anything in my mouth that's not food.

"That's nasty." I tell her and I don't want to. She tells me to do it anyway. I say "No". I don't want to do it.

She won't leave me alone. Keeps telling me to do it while shushing me and grabbing me by my arm so I don't leave the room. I know it's something we can get in trouble for because she's shushing me. She starts trying to force me and I finally do it.

Then she jumps up because she starts to pee on herself. She grabs her shorts and runs to the bathroom. I'm confused, embarrassed and mad at the same time.

Mad because she just made me do that and I didn't want to. I wanna scrub my mouth. Now I'm feeling bad and embarrassed, but I don't know why I feel this way. I know I just did something wrong.

I'm so embarrassed. More upset than anything though. I don't even want to look at her. I don't want to be around her. I don't want to talk to anybody about it. Not even to my daddy when he picks me up and not when I go back home to my mom's.

I go back home as if nothing had ever happened. It still bothers me though. I didn't wanna do that.

CHAPTER 3

Party Upstairs

We move to a big white house with an attic on 22nd Street. You walk into a small open area with a fireplace. Stairs to the left with a closet and window at the bottom of the stairs.

You can go up those stairs to a landing that leads directly down another set of stairs to the kitchen and to the right of the landing you go up the stairs to the second level.

To the right of the entry is an opening to the living room and off the living room to the left is the formal dining room. Back door off the kitchen with a small back porch.

We have a big fenced in backyard with rhubarb along the side of the fence. After we pick and clean the rhubarb we pour a little salt on it and eat it. It has a sour taste and gives us the runs, but we eat it again and again anyway.

Up to the second level there's two doors in front of you separated by wall space. They're two adjoining bedrooms. My mom made both these rooms her own. One side is her bedroom and the other is her sitting room.

To the right of the stairs down the small hallway is another bedroom. To the left is a bathroom and a door next to it that opens to the attic stairs. There are two rooms in the attic. That's where my sisters and I sleep.

One car garage attached to the house. Nasty, scary basement that's not even close to being finished. We don't really go down there.

We quickly make new friends on our new block. I become good friends with the boy living directly across the street, his name is Larry. His dad and Anthony already knew each other.

Soon we become friends with all the kids in the neighborhood. Having our own track meets in the middle of the street. Tetherball in the front yard. A very small front yard. Grill right in front of the porch.

With five kids, our house was quickly popular with all the other kids in the neighborhood. We know everybody over here.

My mom and daddy talk now, and I get to go to my daddy's on weekends from her house again. I'm so happy. It's two different worlds. Connie goes with me sometimes. My mom says me, and Connie have the same dad, but I don't believe it. We don't look like we have the same mom and dad.

I also ask my daddy to let Penny go sometimes to play with my Barbie's, and he lets her.

I feel bad leaving her behind and we have a lot of fun playing with my dolls at my daddy's.

After my daddy drops me off at home on Sundays, he goes home and calls me right away. We sit on the phone for hours talking and laughing.

My aunt Jackie comes over and ask who I'm on the phone with. She gets so upset when I tell her it's my daddy. She wants to know what we're talking about and why I'm on the phone for so long.

What could we possibly have to talk about for so long when he just had me for the whole weekend and now he's keeping me from my other family. She doesn't like it at all.

With my mom having all girls my uncles rough us up a little when they come in town, all in good fun. One is a boxer and I like to watch him soak his bruised, busted hands in a sink of Epsom salt after his fights or practice and listen to his stories. Makes me want to be rough and tough like him so I wrestle the boys on the block.

I usually win, making them cry and rubbing it in. I wrestle my male cousins all the time too. I get roughed up; I like to be rough with them.

Plus, my daddy teaches me karate and I'm pretty good at it. Sometimes he gets frustrated 'cause I keep giggling but when he tells me to show him, I do it perfect. He's impressed. I'm paying attention. I just can't stay serious. I'm too silly.

My mom finally breaks up with Anthony and starts dating other guys. I'm about eleven and he pops up while she has company over one day.

The new guy's a lot nicer, but Anthony doesn't care about that. He comes in sniffing my mom. Tells her she smells like sex, then turns and jumps on the new guy knocking him onto the couch, choking him.

The new guy's not much of a fighter at all, so I jump on Anthony's back trying to choke him and scratch his neck.

When Connie pulls me off, I yell "You stupid." That's my curse word. He looks at me and laughs. "It's not funny stupid." My mom's standing by the door scared and crying.

He gets up off the guy and leaves. I was so mad at him for trying to keep my mom from moving on. He's so irritating. I just want somebody to beat him up. I try but I don't think I'm hurting him.

Anyway, new guy must've gotten scared 'cause we didn't see him much after that. Her next friend knows a little karate too. He still wasn't around long though, he fell off quickly like the last one. Anthony probably got to him too.

Now Connie's got a boyfriend. I guess that's what he is and he's so ugly. Big and ugly. Ol' nasty black gums. He tries to get information from me and Penny about Connie, so we charge him.

"Give us a couple dollars and we'll tell you". A couple dollars is a lot to us, and 7-Eleven is right on the corner.

He keeps on paying us even though there isn't much to tell. We make up stories so we can get paid. We're just trying to make a little change.

Oh, and my imagination's not too bad either. With Anthony gone, things are better. My mom's not worried about us being in the house while she's gone. She still fusses at us about the food but it's still better. Eating a lot of syrup sandwiches and cinnamon and sugar toast.

I like sweets so I sneak and cut a tiny line straight across the brownies hoping she won't notice when she gets home. All good, we can relax a little and I can play for hours with my dolls and stuffed animals while she's gone.

Connie sits on the couch watching while I play in the dining room. I set the chairs up like a car and put my dolls in them. We drive to church and when we get to church, we sang in that choir. "Soon and very soon, we are going to see the king."

"I been running for my Jesus for a long time, I'm not tired yet. I'm not tired. I'm not tired yet." Yes, we sang.

I rearrange the chairs from scene to scene, getting into it as Connie watches. She says I should be an actor. It's better than watching TV, I guess.

I love playing with my dolls and collections of Smurfs, My Little Pony, Strawberry Shortcake and Barbie of course. My daddy buys me all the toys I ask for.

I don't really have to share my toys but I do have to share rooms. We don't have a lot of privacy in a house full of girls. Not only do we share clothes, we also have to share the bathroom. It's not uncommon to have more than one of us in the bathroom at the same time.

Penny and I are in the bathroom when we come up with the idea to prank my mom. I'm at the sink while she's on the toilet taking a dump. I tell her to pause and lay toilet paper across the toilet in layers and dookey on it, so she does.

Then we put it in the bathroom cabinet and leave the bathroom to wait on the attic stairs with the door closed.

My mom goes into the bathroom and all of a sudden, she starts yelling. "Who the fuck put this shit in the damn cabinet?" She's pissed. She's going off so hard. Snapping on us. We're on the attic stairs with the door closed cracking up.

She opens the door ready to beat us, but we're laughing so hard we're crying. Seeing us laugh like that she can't help but start laughing herself. Laughter saved us, but we still had to clean it. Well Penny did. I wasn't touching her dookey. Nah, that's just nasty.

Then we do the sneak and peek. We sometimes sit at the top of the stairs peeking through the rails, spying on my mom's parties. The way our stairs are set up we really can't see anything, but we can hear them.

We come up with that "I'm thirsty" excuse to get downstairs and get a closer look, get yelled at and sent right back up the stairs.

We come down the stairs the next morning to one of my mom's close friends passed out drunk on the couch. She crashes on my mom's couch from time to time.

My mom says she feeds her and her daughter a lot. She can't cook and doesn't know how to keep house I guess. Her name is Denise and they've been friends for years, including the time frame my mom and daddy were married. My mom and Denise even work together.

Going with my daddy on the weekends, we start staying over at Denise's place. He loads us all up in the car to ride downtown and scoop the loop. It's the thing to do on weekends. Everybody does it. Natalie comes too. We sit in the backseat mean mugging each other and trying not to let our knees touch each other. Still not getting along.

Now when I get back home to my mom's she's upset and cursing about my daddy and I being at Denise's. I'm a little torn. I don't even know why my mom and daddy are no longer together. I don't remember a time when they were together.

I know they were married because she mentions it and I see the picture of them on their wedding day. Nobody in that picture looked happy at all. It was clearly not a happy occasion.

She said my daddy was crazy but didn't tell me what he did, and I never wanted to ask. I didn't want to get in trouble for asking. My mom doesn't like us asking her questions.

I thought Denise was alright, we didn't have any problems, but I began to question how to feel about her because my mom is so upset about her being with my daddy and I'm protective of my mom. She didn't do anything to me but her being with my daddy is upsetting my mom.

I'm not fully understanding the whole situation, but I know Denise is doing something wrong and now her and my mom can't be friends anymore. It must be bad for friends to hang out with the same guy.

Still, weekends with my daddy and Denise aren't too bad. It's cramped in the little apartment but I like it better than being at my mom's most of the time. I'm not getting beat or cursed out. I still love my mom, but that house is crazy.

My daddy takes us places, does fun things with us, and always compliments me. We have to go to church every Sunday. Bible study and choir rehearsal every week. I've never been a singer, but my daddy was brought up in the church and keeps us going whenever we're with him. He's head Deacon.

His mom, dad, brothers, and sisters go to the same church. The ones that still live in town. I don't mind it, although most of the time I feel like I don't belong. I feel so out of place. They seem so different from me and what I'm used to. It doesn't look real to me.

I feel that way at just about every family function with my daddy's side of the family. Some tease me for calling my dad, daddy.

He tells me my grandma doesn't like me and that's where he was staying before moving in with Denise. I walked over one freezing cold morning before school to get a ride but my daddy wasn't home.

My grandma said he went out for coffee and closed the door in my face. My feelings were hurt. I couldn't believe she didn't let me in as cold as it is outside.

My daddy must've been telling the truth, she doesn't like me.

I sat on the cold front step waiting for my daddy to come back. When he pulled up, he asked why I was outside in the cold and not waiting inside. I told him that grandma closed the door right after telling me he wasn't home.

He was upset that she left me in the cold and fussed at her, yet we go to a celebration at her house every Christmas Eve. They have a big pot of chili on the stove every year with some other side dishes and sweets.

They pass around Christmas song books. Everybody has to gather around and sing from these books. I don't like it. Secret Santa gifts.

Denise gets upset that there aren't any gifts for us. She told my daddy if that doesn't change she's not coming anymore. We're the only kids not receiving gifts over here on Christmas Eve. It's not fair that we have to watch everybody else open gifts and none for us. Most of them have a really light skin tone and thin curly hair. All the men in my daddy's generation have the bozo the clown balding.

We always go to Denise's parents' house after leaving my grandma's. It's warm and cozy. There's more food and a smaller but closer gathering. They have gifts for all of us. I feel more comfortable with her family.

Even though my daddy spoils me, every now and then I get him a little upset. I love scary movies. Poltergeist is one of my favorites. I've watched it several times.

So, I'm in the car with my daddy, Connie and one of our cousins and I'm sitting in the front passenger seat. We're driving past the cemetery and it reminds me of the part of Poltergeist where the little girl's bird died.

They put the bird in a shoe box and buried it out in the backyard. Later the little boy asks if they can dig up the dead bird to see it's bones.

Again, I love movies. So, as we're driving by the cemetery, I ask my daddy if we can go dig up my sister's bones. I'm just following what I saw in the movie. My daddy has no words. He does, however, slap the hell out of me. Back hand to the mouth.

Well damn!

As I turn around to look in the backseat, Connie and my cousin are back there trying so hard not to let my daddy hear them laughing.

Guess that was a dumb thing to say!

The rest of the ride was real quiet. So different from home to home. I don't have to clean everything at my daddy's. I'm a spoiled brat and I can eat whatever's there whenever I want. I complained to my daddy that we were out of clean bath towels.

Denise looks at me with this half grin and says, "Well maybe you should wash some."

I looked at her and my daddy and said, "No I'm not, that's your job." My daddy just said, "Come on you guys."

Then to my moms, where I feel like I'm in the way at times. Like she just wants a man and the youngest child. Me and my other sisters always feel she puts men ahead of us. Always takes their side over ours.

As for holidays with my mom, we don't have the traditional Christmas party. We do sometimes have company for Thanksgiving at home and everybody loves gatherings at Grandma Delia's in Fort Dodge.

A big house overlooking the railroad tracks with a whore house next door. We always hear stories about the whores next door when we go there. Then you see them coming in and out the side door.

The whole family comes to Grandma's. When the kids act up, Grandma Delia sends us out to the back yard to pick our own switch.

Trying to be slick and pick a twig only makes our whoopin worse, but somebody has to try it anyway. Then run circles around the dining room table. We know she can't catch us. She's old, so she'll give up and catch us slippin later.

Always great times though.

The house is so old. You can feel parts of the floor sinking in when you walk. Some parts are slanted, holes in the bottom of the walls here and there. We don't care. It's Grandma's house. Family time.

Plenty of blankets and house coats. If you don't bring church clothes my grandma will make you put on one of her house coats for church and you already know everybody's gonna be laughing at you in Grandma Delia's moo moo.

No talking and laughing in church or you'll get popped with that paddle or her slipper. Grandma's not playing!

I have my share of fun at my mom's too though. When I'm not having to babysit for her friends. I don't like little kids and I'm not good with them. One of her friends has a baby. I don't know why my mom told her I could watch this baby. She won't stop crying and I don't know what to do with her. Getting real annoyed with all the noise, I start shaking her trying to shut her up.

Ugh, she's getting on my nerves.

Luckily my mom is still home. She comes running down the stairs snatching the baby from me. Says you're not supposed to shake a baby. Well, I don't know nothing about no baby, and I don't want to watch her. *Call her momma.*

I'm in middle school around this time. I love slumber parties. My mom leaves and makes Connie watch us. She usually has one of her friends over to help her and I've had the same group of friends since elementary.

Being a January baby, we get to play in the snow as well as drive my sister crazy. She yells at us all night, but we don't care. We're loud and annoying. Blah, blah, blah.

Connie and I still fight. I said I don't believe we have the same dad and we get into it every time I ask how we have the same mom and dad yet look so different. I just find it hard to believe and hard to let go.

She calls me an evil, selfish little bitch all the time. She gets so mad at me for bringing it up. I ask my daddy about it, but I can't get a straight answer. I really want to know. I don't believe it.

I'm not trying to upset Connie, maybe she really does believe it. I just can't accept it and so we fight. Every single time it turns physical. I'm not trying to start a fight.

I guess I should be asking my mom, but I'm not trying to deal with whatever her response is gonna be. *Mm Mm.*

I'll pass.

I know she won't answer. She'll probably slap me for asking. Hell, I got yelled at once for telling her the food was good and asking how she made it. *Nah!* Not gonna do that.

My mom keeps having parties, but they start to change up. Like secret parties behind closed doors in those two adjoining rooms she has to herself.

Connie went into her room one day and found a lunchbox with white powder in a bag.

Uh oh, could it be candy?

She didn't know what it was, so she took it to school to ask a friend and he knew exactly what it was. When my mom finds out what Connie did, she sends her away.

Months later, I go to church one Sunday with my daddy and see Connie there. I don't know how she got there, but she looks different. She gained a lot of weight while staying at Orchard Place. She was so big I thought it was a costume.

I had to poke her belly to see. It wasn't cotton stuffing. She really gained weight. I felt sorry for her. I don't know much about the place. All I know is that bad kids go there. I'm happy to see her though. She comes back to the house and we're back to fighting.

I go out and play with my friends to escape the madness in my house. We break into empty houses to hang out as our clubhouses.

Larry and I hang out a lot. He pops up to see me soon as I get back from my daddy's one day. My daddy did my hair and I have no time to fix the mess he made in my head.

I walk out to the porch and Larry just falls out laughing. I'm so embarrassed.

I swear to never let my daddy do my hair ever again.

I run in the house and yank the ponytail holders out immediately.

My daddy made me look ugly as hell.

CHAPTER 4

Wedding Bells

There's talk of a wedding

My daddy's gonna marry Denise and I'm supposed to be in the wedding. Every time I'm supposed to go with my daddy for rehearsal my mom says I can't. She doesn't want me at any of the rehearsals or the wedding. I'm not really upset though.

How much fun could a wedding be for me?

After they get married, they move to a house on School Street and my daddy gets a vasectomy soon after. He doesn't want any more kids and Denise is okay with that. Whew! No more sisters.

I'm so happy they moved, and we have a lot more space. There's a bedroom with my own bed to sleep in now when I stay over. It has two twin beds in it. One for me and one for Natalie. Small but it'll do.

I turn the basement into my Barbie world. There's two large rooms. One with carpet and wood panel walls and the other is the laundry room. My friends and younger sisters by my mom come over to play with me sometimes.

We love playing with all my doll collections. Including my whole Smurf village. My collections keep us busy for hours.

For my slumber parties, we play games and Barbie's of course. My favorite. I have a Barbie house, pool, cars and a wardrobe closet. Plenty to keep us busy.

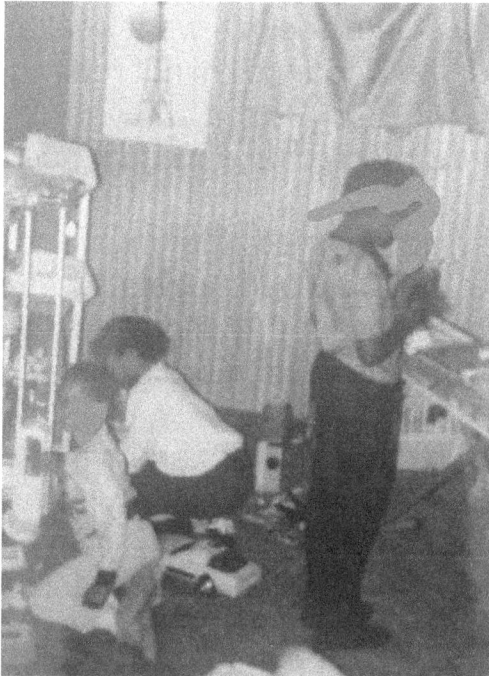

I love music too. My daddy has an 8-track player on the stereo in the basement and in his car. The car is a clean, green, two-door Buick. My friends, sisters and I go down to the basement to turn up the music and sing.

Mariah Carey comes out with this high pitched voice and we be down in the basement screaming, trying our hardest to hit that high note to that and Betty Wright's song, No Pain.

We listen to Shirley Murdock, Teddy P, Peabo Bryson, Luther Vandross and others like them. I'm a big fan of New Kids on the Block (went to a concert), Tigra and Bunny, Salt 'n' Peppa, George Michael, Madonna, Mary J Blige, SWV and Dianna Ross, just to name a few.

After our mini concert, we go upstairs and see my daddy and Denise sitting on the couch, trying to watch TV. Denise looks so annoyed from having to hear our loud mouths screaming for hours.

Sleepovers here are so fun. We get into a cardboard box and slide down the basement stairs right into the wall at the bottom. One of the girls flips out the box at the bottom and hits that wall with her forehead.

She's crying for real and we're crying because we can't stop laughing. That was her last slide. I love hanging out in the basement except for the crickets that come out and run me up the stairs every single time. I hate bugs.

At school I can be a class clown. A couple of my teachers can't stand me for that. I know they get irritated with me but that's okay. My science teacher really gets annoyed by me. The class is boring.

He gives a speech and at the end he looks around at all the bored faces and says, "What, no ooh's and aah's?"

So, I sing, "Ohhhhh aah oh," out loud. The whole class laughs, and he rolls his eyes at me.

Well that's what ya wanted, ain't it!

My three best friends are Lena, Shania and Malayna who live close by. I met Lena in middle school. She has a tire swing in her front yard that we love to pile up on together, even in the winter.

We can play on this tire for hours, getting dusted. Falling off, getting knocked off, accidently swinging into the tree. Her parents are married and two little sisters that are always following us, lurking in corners. Lena's so into WWE that she gets mad anytime we tell her it's fake and it turns into an argument.

Shania lives with her mom, older brother and two older sisters. Feels like family with them. They seem to be close to each other, really sticking together, having each other's backs, and making me feel like family.

She's a tomboy and beating up on all the boys, like me. We're always laughing and being silly together. We've been friends since elementary.

Malayna's been my friend since elementary too. She lives with her mom, older brother and younger sister. We play with Barbie's on her front porch when the weather's nice.

We all go to the same middle school with a few classes together and call ourselves the Brat Pack. One day in gym class; Shania's trying to tell me something from across the gym. Pointing at me and then at her shirt.

I look down at my shirt and from the lighting of the gym, I can see my balls of toilet paper in my training bra plain as day. I think I'm the only girl in the school without boobs and teased for it all the time. Girls put me on blast and laugh at my flat chest.

I still want the training bras because all the other girls have them, so my daddy got me some. My cousin told me that toilet paper in your bra makes your boobs grow, so I did it. Now I'm stuck.

I can't take the toilet paper out in front of everybody and it doesn't look like anybody's noticed it yet' so I'm trying to turn away from the class. Even though you could see it in the gym, I keep it in there the whole day anyway. A big mistake.

Larry comes over when I get home and my mom comes out the porch and yanks my toilet paper out saying, "What's this." He starts laughing immediately.

Thanks mom.

On top of being teased at school, some of my mom's friends tease me for being so skinny and the fact that I can't find a pair of jeans to fit tight on my long skinny legs. Long, skinny and flat chested with lots of hair. That's ok though.

My daddy still makes me feel special. He always tells me how pretty I am and how others tell him how pretty his daughter is. He got me a black onyx ring for Valentine's day and I don't take it off for anything.

CHAPTER 5

Daddy's Girl

Not long after my daddy and Denise moved, I end up moving in with them because my mom gets lost on drugs.

She drops us off with a friend and doesn't come back for us. That's how I end up living with my daddy at twelve years old. Connie eventually comes to stay with us too.

With my mom, I caught the school bus and winter was torture. My scarf would stick to my face by the frozen snot, the cold freezing my jerry curl.

I tried to move some of the hair from my face, but it was so cold the curl was frozen and broke right off. My little curl landed in the snow and my friend at the bus stop thought it was so funny.

Staying with my daddy, he drives me to school. Every morning, he wakes me up for school and then goes to lie back down in his bed. I get myself together and go to his room to let him know when I'm ready.

This is about the time Denise gets up and takes her turn in the bathroom. We only have one. I usually sit next to him on the side of the bed waiting for him to move. Once he gets ready to get up, I head downstairs to get my shoes on and wait for him to come down. That's our routine.

This morning, he wakes me up and goes back to his room as usual. Denise gets up and goes to the bathroom when I go to get him up. I sit on the edge of the bed waiting for him to get up.

Instead of getting up, he pulls me onto the bed, so I lay down next to him.

He must not be ready to get up.

Then he rolls me over on top of him.

As I'm lying on top of him, he grabs my butt holding onto me and starts moving his hips up and down against mine.

"Daddy, what are you doing?"

He doesn't say anything, so I just lay there feeling weird as he keeps doing it. I don't know what my daddy's doing.

He pushes me off when we hear the bathroom door open telling me to go downstairs, so I walk past Denise in silence. I'm walking out of the room as she's coming in.

At this point it's normal for us to pass by each other without speaking. Our relationship has changed. She doesn't seem to like me much anymore. She loves Natalie though. They're like besties.

My daddy told me that her and her daughter were jealous of our relationship and she always complains about the things he does for me. He does too much for me and not enough for her and her daughter.

I wait on the couch for my daddy to come down and take me to school. When he comes downstairs, we walk outside and get into the car in silence.

When we get close to the school, he says to me, "You know that was your fault. You better not tell anybody."

Tell what?

I don't even know what happened back at the house, but I know it was uncomfortable. I know it didn't feel right and I know it must not be right, because he stopped when he heard Denise coming.

Things have felt a little awkward between us since that morning. I don't know what to think or how to be around my daddy. I don't know if I did something wrong. I don't know if I should sit next to him on the bed in the mornings. I don't want to sit on his bed now because maybe that's why he did that. I stand now.

After a little time goes by, we're home alone one day when he calls me into his room where he's standing naked and smiling.

I don't like seeing my daddy like this. He tells me to take my pants and underwear off and lay down on the floor. He keeps smiling like this is a fun game we're playing.

I don't know what to think. All I know is this is my daddy. The only one who does good things for me, acts like he cares and takes care of me.

Nobody else in this house likes me, so I have to play my daddy's game.

As he gets on top of me, he starts moving his hips up and down again. Then he reaches his hand down between our legs and puts his private part inside me. It hurts, but I don't say anything.

He says I feel as good as my mom. He tells me God says there's nothing wrong when it comes to having sex.

So that's what we're doing!

He's the deacon who knows the Bible, not me and I don't know anything about sex.

Even though God says this is okay for us to do, he tells me I still can't tell anybody, says no one will believe me and I'll get in trouble for saying those things about my daddy.

He told me a story about a coworker. This guy's penis is as big as his forearm, so I go to school and tell Malayna the story about the coworker.

She turns her nose up at me and asks why my daddy would tell me something like that. I don't understand why she thinks it's so bad.

Even though I'm uncomfortable with what's going on, my daddy says God said there's nothing wrong with it. I haven't read the Bible, so I don't know for myself and no one's ever talked to me about sex.

No one talked to me about what the Bible says about sex nor about my body and what I'm supposed to do with it. I want to trust my daddy though and he's a deacon in the church.

As time goes on and this thing with my daddy goes on, I start feeling different, yet I don't know why. He tells me he doesn't like doing this with Denise because he's turned off by her roles when she takes her clothes off. She's not model size.

After leaving a family get together, he says one of our guy cousins told him he couldn't see how my daddy could keep his hands off me. This guy said it would be hard to resist.

I don't understand what's going on now. I don't understand why my cousin would talk about me that way, but I guess it's normal.

My daddy talks to me now like I'm his best friend. It's so different now. It feels different. I sit in the back of the church now. I don't want to be around any of these people. I don't want them to talk to me or hug me.

My daddy starts coming down to the basement while I'm playing with my Barbie's after everyone else goes to bed, so he can do the things with me that he doesn't want to do with Denise.

When I stop playing in the basement at night, he starts taking me down there anyway when everyone else goes to bed.

Denise never comes down looking for him. I start to wish she would. I don't want to do this anymore, but I don't want to hurt my daddy's feelings and get him upset with me.

He made me get on my knees and put it in my mouth in the kitchen one night. Then something came out of the tip. Something slimy and funny tasting. When I jumped up and started spitting it out in the sink, he laughed.

I start getting nervous when Denise leaves me at home with him or at night while everyone is asleep, 'cause I don't know when he's gonna come get me.

After a while though, it's like I'm not in my body when he's doing this to me. It's like I'm hanging on the ceiling looking down at myself. I go numb. I have to go somewhere else until he's finished. I just disappear from my body. When he's done, I go clean myself up while he goes to bed.

I have to stay home from school for a few days after getting my tonsils out. I stay on the pull-out sofa in the living room. He's upstairs, Denise is at work and her daughter's at school. He comes running downstairs naked and excited.

I'm tired and in a little pain, so I tell him I don't want to do it. His response?! He smiles and says he's proud of me for speaking up.

What?
Why?
Really?

This is what you say to me rightnow!

You're proud of me for telling you I don't want to do this, yet I know it won't stop you for good. You don't apologize for ruining me in the first place.
You show no remorse at all. How do you stand there and say some stupid ass shit like this to me?

I just wanna cry; You took my innocence.

I get a little upset by his response, but of course I can't say that to him. As this thing has gone on, I've started to learn a little more about sex from hearing friends talk about it and little things on TV.

He made it seem like a game at first. As if we were really doing something good and fun. Just me and my daddy, because he's always treating me special, but it didn't feel good or fun. I don't understand his thoughts on this.

I just want to hurt him sometimes. I've never felt this way about him. This is my dad! He's been everything to me. I'm not supposed to think this way.

I'm supposed to love him like he's supposed to love me. He's also supposed to protect me from harm.

So why do I damn near feel hate for him and see disgust when I look at him right now?!

A short while later as he continued this thing, he got too rough. Today I'm in a lot of pain. My lower stomach hurts bad from the inside, so he takes me to the doctor and stays in the room while the doctor examines me.

Maybe he stays in the room to make sure I don't tell the doctor anything he doesn't want me to tell. The doctor looks at my dad with this look of, "your daughter is a whore," and tells my dad that I've been ruptured down there.

Like, "your daughters out screwing little boys."

My dad has this stupid ass look on his face. Of course he doesn't stand up for me and say, "Oh that's my fault." Doesn't assure the doctor it's not my fault. Let's the man think I'm just too damn fast.

He writes a prescription for pain meds and sends us out the door. We get in the car and my dad is apologizing for rupturing me. I know he's not going to stop though.

He's only sorry that what he did led me to the doctor and our little secret was close to getting out.

Not sorry for doing it in the first place. For making me feel whatever this is I'm feeling.

I sit in my room with a pair of scissors. Thinking about what's going on. I open the scissors and start sliding one sharp edge of the scissors across the outer edge of my hand, staring into space.

Then comes a day when I have the scissors and do it again. This time I press a little harder and I can feel the blade. I look down and see a few cuts in my skin. They're not very deep. Just sliced the skin a little.

My dad walks in and catches me, gets upset and snatches the scissors away from me, yells at me for being stupid and leaves my room.

I go sit in the living room with Connie and our cousin Thelma, they ask if my dad has ever touched me. I don't know where the question came from, but I said

"Yes" and put my head down.

There was a moment of silence and an "I kinda thought so."

Not much of a discussion afterwards nor any help. They just say they had a feeling, but that was it. They didn't say anything else about it to me or anyone else or do anything.

We start having family meetings. Lots of complaints. There are two sofas and one loveseat in the living room. No matter which sofa I sit on, I always sit alone on that sofa.

Everyone else sits together and every problem that everyone has is about me, except Connie. Everyone's against me.

My dad has already told me they all talk about me behind my back. I'm rude, mean and selfish. They don't like me. Even complain about me not wanting to eat at the table with everyone else.

Knowing how they all feel about me, why would I! After a while, I stopped caring. I don't want to be bothered with any of them. I don't care to fix anything.

Everybody hates me and that's fine.
I wouldn't give a damn!

Can't even say at least I have my daddy anymore.

You think I care about all your damn complaints?
Shit!
Hell no!
Fuck y'all!

I start looking at other fathers out with their daughters and wonder if they're doing the same thing to their daughter. Especially when he touches her.

57

I see a little girl holding her dad's hand and I look at her face and then at his and wonder if her dad is doing the same to her. I wonder if she's okay.

I don't know the right way a father-daughter relationship is supposed to look like. I don't know how we're really supposed to act, so I grab his hand and he tells me not to do that. Says people will wonder what's going on. They'll know what we're doing.

I'm so damn lost and confused.
What the hell??
How am I supposed to behave?
What's normal?
What's not?

That little girl is over there sitting on her dad's lap. "Should she be doing that?"

I just sit and watch other people wondering what's going on in their home. I don't know if those girls are going through the same thing. I want to ask if they're dad is touching their privates, but I don't.

Now my body starts changing. All of a sudden I have boobs. Big boobs. I go from being flat chested last school year to having big, perky, perfect boobs the next school year.

I use those words to describe my boobs, 'cause that's what the boys in school say to me. Now I get teased for my big boobs, not my flat chest.

By the time I get to high school, they are huge. My dad's brothers yell, "six o'clock" when I walk in the room. From the front I'm so skinny. Straight up and down with no curves. Turn me sideways and you can't miss these things. Big DDD's on 120 lbs. and 5'5. Sometimes I walk through the halls with my head down crying from being teased about my big boobs. I tell the principal about the kids teasing me and he acts as if I'm bothering him, "Just go to class Neesha."

I start my period and have no clue how to handle it, so I run downstairs to tell my dad and Denise. She gives me a mean look letting me know she doesn't give a damn. I don't know how to deal with it, so my dad runs out to get me some pads.

Then I'm out with Connie and I run out of pads, so she tells me to use a tampon. I don't know what to do with this thing and she didn't tell me how.

I go stick it up there and now I'm walking funny. When Connie and her friends ask me what's wrong, I tell them the tampon hurts. Connie asks how I put it in, so I tell her I just stuck it up there. They start laughing.

I stuck the whole thing up there and left it. Cardboard and all. I didn't know a piece of it was supposed to be pulled off.

Life is still going on for everyone else.

I'm fourteen and Connie's pregnant. I'm so excited and can't wait to see my niece. I want to skip school to be at the hospital for the birth, but my dad won't let me. It's all I can think about all day in school.

When she comes home from the hospital I spend as much time as I can with my niece, Nya. I love her so much. I hold onto her so much that she thinks I'm her mom.

Now that Connie has a baby she decides to move out. I'm sad to see her go. I don't want them to leave me. I ask my dad to take me over there all the time and I keep Nya some weekends.

When my dad won't take me, I'll walk to go see her. I'm on my way to see her one evening and find them in the park near her apartment. It's getting dark, so I'm mad and yelling at Connie for having Nya in that park so late. Her and her friends think it's funny that I'm fussing. I take my niece and leave.

I don't play when it comes to her. She doesn't need to be out there at night. They still have basketball games going on. They sometimes fight in the park. I don't want my niece getting caught in the middle of anybody's fight, so I take her home with me.

Even though I'm crazy about Nya, I never want to have kids of my own nor get married. Nya and my dolls help me escape what's goin on. A little.

My dolls won't stop him from touching me, but he doesn't do it when I have Nya around. Without her here my dad is doing what he wants to me as often as he can.

Now at least I have Nya. She gives me something else.

I love her.

CHAPTER 6

They're Looking

Being in high school and trying to hide this huge secret is scary.

I start seeing the guys a little different. All of a sudden I know longer want to wrestle. I'm noticing how they're looking at me and it makes me a little nervous. I never thought about the way they looked at me before. Never wondered what they were thinking or what they wanted.

Now I know I had a little crush here and there in elementary and middle school. I saw a cute boy, he saw me. We would send notes back and forth, "Do you like me? Check yes or no." That was it. It was fun and cute to hit them and run, but things are different now. Different now because I lost my virginity. I'm not innocent anymore and I feel dirty.

I'm not sure how to take all this attention and I'm afraid I won't be able to keep them off me like my dad.

Some of my friends and these other kids in high school are already having sex with each other because it's what they want to do. They actually like it. Will I be expected to do it now too? I'm sure I will.

I'm not okay with all this but I have to pretend I am. It's a lot to take in. There are a lot of moments where I'm uncomfortable around the guys and girls, but I don't want anybody to know this. Don't want them to make fun of me.

I already feel like they're judging me with their eyes. Like they can just look at me and see how dirty I am. I try to hide my feelings and with that they call me "stuck up" a lot.

Some say I walk around school with my nose in the air. I'm not trying to be mean or stuck up. I just don't want to make eye contact because I feel like if I look them in the eye, they can see everything that's going on with me and they'll talk bad about me.

They won't like me. I don't want them to see it. I'm going crazy inside every day, wondering what they're looking at and why. What are they thinking? I can't talk to anybody.

Even my appetite starts changing. I'm not eating as much. My dad will ask me why.

"I'm not hungry."

He speaks to the principal and counselor about it. They speak to me about it and at this point I'm diagnosed by them as anorexic.

They want me to start seeing the counselor until I start eating more. I'm not doing that. I don't feel my lack of eating is a problem. I don't want to gain weight and I'm not hungry. I see nothing wrong with that,

I'm mainly obsessed with having a flat stomach. That's a huge deal for me. I have to look a certain way. I don't want anybody talking bad about me like my dad talks about Denise.

I stay after school one day for a class project. Once It's done, I go to the front of the school to hang out and wait for my dad to come and get me.

There are other kids hanging out in the student center and the front of building. Some running through the halls, just messing around. A fat kid that I know runs up and grabs me being playful. He wrestles me down onto the bench and lays on top of me, laughing and holding me down.

It scares the hell out of me, and I scream, trying to push him off me as a tear runs down one side of my face.

He gets up running, still laughing and playing. He didn't see the tear. What he thought was a harmless joke scared me for real. I wipe my face and fight back the tears when I get up and walk off in the other direction to pull myself together in a hurry. Before anyone notices I cried for real.

Trying to fit in, I go through a phase of wearing make-up because I see other girls in school doing it. Maybe this will help me blend in.

My dad doesn't like it after a while even though I got the money from him to buy it, so he throws it away. He also has a problem with my underwear. While bringing up the laundry he notices my underwear and tells me I can't buy that type of underwear or the people working at the store will get suspicious.

They'll know I'm having sex because of the underwear I buy. They may even know who it's with according to him. I got the underwear when I went to the mall with my friends.

My friends and I like to play dress up and take pictures. Since I have a 110 camera the film has to be developed by the store photo department, my dad picks up the film and looks through the pics with me.

He tells me I can't take pictures in my swimsuit or some of my poses because the guy developing the film is looking at him crazy when he picks it up. He says I can get him in trouble. I have to be careful with everything I do or people will know.

I have the opportunity to go to Barbizon Modeling and Acting School. I heard about it through school and asked my dad to take me.

I always walk and sit with my back straight up. Some of the kids laugh at me because even when sitting in the student center rocking to the music, my back is still straight.

They ask, "How can you dance with your back straight?"

"I don't know, I just do."

Always watching my posture without realizing it. A few people brought it to me, so my dad and I take the tour and do the paperwork, but my dad changes his mind at the last second. Says he doesn't want any of the men there touching me.

He frowns at any interaction with me and the opposite sex no matter their age. He tells me that seeing me with another boy or man would make him jealous and upset.

Sometimes when I hang out at Lena's house, she has boys there and her parents are fine with it. They're even allowed in her bedroom. My dad definitely won't allow that. Lena's dad is in the home and everything seems fine.

I do catch myself wondering about him from time to time, but I try not to think about it. Lena and her sisters seem fine. They all look happy and comfortable around each other.

I take Penny with me to Lena's sometimes even though my friends and I are in high school and Penny is still in middle school. Sometimes Lena brings her little sisters when we go hang out at the mall or parks.

As time goes by, we're all getting a little bit older and we're meeting so many new kids and our circles slowly began to change. These friends I hung with for so long started making other friends and I did too.

I started going to parties at the downtown YMCA and the Wilkie House. The parties are fun. I walk around and dance. My dad drops me off and picks me up.

I'm meeting new people and making new friends. With all these new friends and hanging out, I start to think about girl talk. I think about the conversations I see in movies when the girls have sleepovers or just hanging out and they talk about their first kiss and losing their virginity.

I'm afraid of that conversation for obvious reasons. How would I respond in that instance? I can't tell the truth.

That's not the cute story they're looking for, so I hope it never comes up with me around, but it does.

I say I lost my virginity to a boy in Fort Dodge. That's it. I change the subject right after, so they don't ask for details.

I'm not a good liar and I know if they ask for more details, I won't be able to make up something on the spot. I'll get too uncomfortable and they'll know I'm know I'm lying or fibbing, as we're supposed to say.

Lying is a bad word according to my mom, her mom and my aunts and uncles. You can also say telling a tale but that's just too much to say. Not even supposed to say butt, supposed to say backside or rear. Anyways, kids don't talk like that when grownups aren't around.

Hanging out at Ruby's place, I meet a guy around my age named Will. He hardly ever speaks to me, just stares at me a lot, him, and his cousin.

They stare and mumble to each other. I overhear him talking to his cousin about the gap in between my legs.

He says, "yeah, she been doing something, look at that gap between her legs."

I pretend not to hear it 'cause it's awkward and it hurt my feelings. I didn't get the gap on purpose. I didn't have a choice, it's not my fault. I can't even defend myself.

I mean what can I possibly say to that? I have no response.

I keep my back turned to them and keep looking towards the TV as if I ain't heard nothing at all.

He eventually speaks to me but it's still not much and I can't say much 'cause I'm too shy and it's awkward.

I still continue to hang out at Ruby's anyway. It's better than being in the house with my dad and trying to dodge those moments in the house alone with him.

I was just playing with my dolls and now I'm expected to be a grown up doing grown up things. Walking around with a gap between my legs that everyone know I'm having sex.

No way to deny it.

I'm not ready for this but I know I need to grin and bear it. Tune it out and be silly me. I can do that, and high school won't be so bad.

I go to the dances and enjoy myself laughing and dancing with friends. I'm in the moment. I'll enjoy where I'm at right now and not think about that.

CHAPTER 7

Nowhere to Hide

My dad is diabetic, and it starts to progress. I don't feel bad for him. When he goes into insulin shock we have to force a spoonful of jelly with added sugar into his mouth or extra sweet Kool-Aid. Being that close to him, having to help him makes me feel disgusted.

Why should I help him?

Sometimes I want to jab the spoon down his throat when I have to touch his face. Grab him and hold his face still to get the spoon in his mouth. Sometimes forcing his mouth open.

Why can't I just look the other way?
What's the worst that can happen to him if I just leave the room?

Still, I do what I'm supposed to do. I'm his daughter so I have to help him. Although it didn't matter to him that I'm his daughter when he hurt me. Still, I do my part.

I hate the smell of his breath. I had to ask him why his breath still stinks after brushing his teeth. It's because of his diabetes. The sickness in his body causes his breath to stink.

He has to give himself insulin shots in his leg daily and It's because of his health that he's forced into an early retirement that he's not happy about at all.

He's been on that job a long time and loves the money it brings in. Always talks about all the money he's leaving me in his Will. I don't know why he brings it up so much but he does. Maybe that's supposed to make me feel better. Make up for what he's done to me.

Being in early retirement, he has to find other ways to fill his mornings. He meets up with his brothers for coffee at McDonald's and goes to his parent's house.

His dad is sick and has been in a wheelchair for a while, they put him into a home. The family is called to the home cause he's not doing good. They're all here, but I have homework and want to get home.

Soon as my dad gets me to the house, Denise calls and tells my dad he needs to get back. Soon as we walk into the house, they tell us my grandfather passed away and my dad collapses.

I don't know a whole lot about my grandfather, but I remember seeing him run up and down the aisle in church shouting and praising God. Then he was in the wheelchair sick. I don't know what he had.

With my dad's health getting worse, I'm able to get away from the house more. I get my driver's license and he lets me drive his new van.

I love the freedom of being able to drive around on my own. I go pick up my friends on the way to parties at the Y or just go hang out at a friend's house.

After one night out, I get in the van with my dad and he notices the small window in the back is open. He immediately gets upset and ask why I was in the back of the van.

I was at a friend's place last night and before I left, we sat in the back of the van kissing. Now my dad knows. He's looking at me with this crazy look in his eyes that's scaring me. I told him the truth. He's fussing at me but he doesn't hit me. I was scared 'cause I thought he would. Instead, I lost my driving privilege.

I still get to go to Connie and Ruby's for overnight stays though. Will and his cousin are getting a little more comfortable and speak a little more. It's better that he's talking instead of him just staring at me all the time.

He even asks for my number, not knowing if I have a choice, I give it to him. He calls and wants to visit me at my dad's and my dad's okay with it. I'm surprised.

He walks over through the cold and snow dragging his cousin with him. My dad's impressed that he would take that long, cold walk to see me and we both had respect for Will after that. For that, he was allowed to hang out for a little while. We even got to go to the basement. We talked and listened to music until my dad came down and told them it was time to leave.

As winter lets up, I get out and about on foot. Walking with Nya, she falls asleep in my arms and I happen to see my mom sitting on a concrete wall along the sidewalk. Excited to see her and introduce her to her granddaughter for the first time.

I walk up, "Mom, this is Nya, your granddaughter."

She won't even look at her. She can barely look at me, she's so high. She looks all around me as if she's trying to avoid me.

I'm so mad and lose respect for her. She doesn't even look like herself, so skinny, hair's a mess, skin dark in places, clothes hanging off her.

She doesn't want to talk to me, blows me off. That hurt my feelings. I walk away disappointed in her. I even call her a crackhead when I get back to Connie's. I can't believe what I just saw.

I run into my mom again a while later and she recognizes me. She's not high this time and holds a conversation with me.

Still skinny and seeing the bones sticking out of her chest in her tank top is bothersome.

She tells me about her boyfriend setting the mattress on fire while she was asleep on it and running off at her previous apartment. Luckily, she woke up in time to get out unharmed. Being in and out of jail, she sounds like she's trying to get clean. I can only hope.

I don't like seeing her like this, but I'm happy to see her. Happy she recognizes me and can talk to me as she walks me to her new place: a one-bedroom duplex not far from Connie. Real small. Not much to it at all, but it's hers.

Even though I now know where she stays, I still don't see her much. She doesn't stay put long. I know because I have to pass by that duplex to get to Connie's place.

Connie has these friends she's known for a long time. At least since we lived on 22nd street. It's a big family, but there are three sisters I see a lot and one of their brothers. She's roommates with one of the sisters, so I go over to play with their kids.

I remember when I didn't like playing with smaller kids. One day I visit and the roommate asks me to sit with the kids while she runs out for a minute. As I'm waiting for her to come back, her boyfriend comes in.

It's not uncommon for the door to be unlocked during the day.

He walks in, looks at me then walks through the apartment. Since he's here I don't see the need for me to stay so I'm gonna leave. As I get up to leave, he comes walking real fast from the bedroom and grabs me by my arms, pulling on me.

The kids are just babies so they can only sit and watch, not understanding what's happening. They can't talk yet. I try to yank away from him. I'm trying to pull away, saying "No no no," as he's dragging me down the small hallway to the bedroom.

When we get to the bedroom, he picks me up, slams me onto the bed and jumps on top of me.
I'm still struggling with him when we hear the front door open and he jumps up off me. Points at me with the crazy look in his eyes,

I already know what that means. I quickly walk out the door without saying anything to my sister's friend except, "Bye." Not a word of it to Connie either.

I start spending more time at Ruby's, who doesn't have a roommate. Probably too crazy for one. She's mean, a fighter and a bully with a cute little black and white dog that won't get too big and I love playing with her.

Then there's her upstairs neighbors. A drug addicted couple with a little boy and girl about four and five. The kids come down to play with me and the dog and I've been up to their apartment with Ruby a couple times.

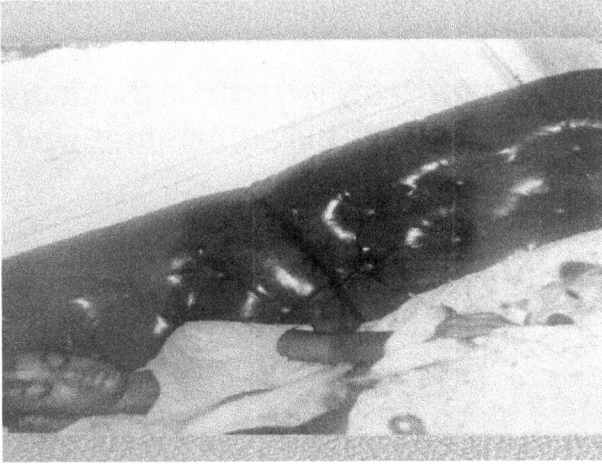

I'm alone in the apartment one day when the neighbor's boyfriend comes walking in. It's common for her to leave her door unlocked too.

When I tell him Ruby's gone, he smiles and starts walking towards me. As I take a few steps back, he continues to walk through the apartment towards Ruby's bedroom. I walk to the hallway and tell him again that she's not home.

Standing in the doorway to her bedroom he tells me to, "come here."

I tell him "No," and start walking towards the front door.

He comes and grabs me by one arm pulling me to the bedroom.

I keep yelling, "No, let me go!" While he's pulling my right arm, I have my left arm on the doorway trying to keep from being pulled all the way into the bedroom.

All of a sudden, we hear, "Hey, what's going on in here?"

The guy stops pulling on me and we see Will and his cousin standing in the hallway.

Thank God!

The guy takes off running past Will and his cousin and out the door.

Even though I can't speak or even look at Will or his cousin right now, I'm so glad they walked in when they did and happy at that time that the door was unlocked. Grateful they saved me.

I walk past them with my head down and sit on the couch.

I don't speak a word of it to Ruby. I've never spoken to the guy before this day and barely looked at him when Ruby took me up to their apartment.

I don't know what made him do it, but I'm going back to my dad's.

Doesn't seem to matter where I am, men keep coming after me.

What did I do?

CHAPTER 8

Perceptions of Darkness

In the midst of my darkness, what did everyone else see? While I was in the dark, they saw the light.

I know this because I went back and asked a few people who knew me back then. This was an assignment from the therapist I'm currently seeing. She suggested I go and ask a couple of my close friends what they thought of me back then, how they saw me.

In my mind, I thought people were looking down on me. I thought everyone thought the worst of me and that very few really liked me. I thought they saw me as a bad person.

I felt alone, hurt, and broken inside. I didn't feel like I could talk to anyone about my feelings or what was really going on. I thought no one would believe me or care to hear it.

It would be his word against mine and they don't believe the kids. He told me they wouldn't believe me. So I held it in.

When I recently sat down with Denise, I could feel the tension. I knew she was nervous and unsure of what was about to happen.

When I smiled at her and assured her that I had nothing against her, I saw her shoulders relax and I could tell she felt a little better, but still unsure of why I would be asking her to meet me.

I told her about the book and me seeing a therapist. I told her that I was struggling with my past. A past she was unaware of.

She told me she had her suspicions about my dad and what he may have done to me after I had already moved out. Her suspicion only came about when her daughter told her he tried to touch her after I was out of the house.

She went on to tell me that she thought I was mean, rude, very disrespectful, and thought I hated everyone in that house because my dad told her I hated them. It was because of his lies that she didn't care for me and didn't like having me around

After talking with her and learning our truths, she said "He kept us from having a great relationship. He turned us against each other on purpose."

A little late, but we're glad to have finally come together to learn the truth and she's happy I'm able to share my story.

Shania saw a silly little girl who she could count on for laughs and help beating up the boys. Always being silly together. She recalled a night she stayed over.

She laughed as she recalled us waiting for my dad and Denise to go to sleep and us getting dressed and she doing my hair to walk to the gas station around the corner for snacks.

As we were walking out of the gas station, a guy got out of his car and yelled at us, "Hey."

We looked over to the right and there was my dad giving this guy a crazy look. He got right back in his car. My dad snatched me up and told us both to get in the car.

He took Shania back to the house to get her bag and then drove her home. Told her mom we had snuck out, and then we left. He was so upset that night. She never suspected anything was going on though. All she saw was a silly little girl and an overprotective dad. At that point, he had already had his way with me.

When I met up with Malayna she said she was jealous of the relationship I had with my dad. What she saw was a close relationship between father and daughter. He spoiled me and she was jealous and said a lot of others were as well.

Most little girls want that close relationship with their daddy. Typically, when you think of father and daughter you think, daddy's girl. She saw a girl who was happy, yet always ready to fight.

Shell, whom I haven't mentioned yet saw me as bright- eyed, energetic, spontaneous, and ahead of my time. She was nineteen when we met and I was fifteen or sixteen. From what she could see, I didn't have anybody in my corner. She could tell I had been hurt, as she had been through her own battles.

She saw me as the leader of my sisters and saw me as having a lot of responsibility and for years, thought I was older than I really was.

Bobby and I met when I was seventeen. He saw strength and responsibility; he knew I didn't like to fight but I was down to fight when I had to.

A cousin of mine spoke on how my mom always kept our hair done and bought us nice clothes. She made sure we looked good when we went out.

I've had numerous others come to me and tell me they've always admired my strength and the way I carry myself.

There are those who have always called me crazy. Those who say I'm fun to be around. Through it all only two saw pain and of those two they both still saw strength in me.

The image of strength is what stands out to me. Through all the pain I was going through it amazes me that so many saw strength. Through it all I still shined when I thought I was dimming the light.

I am amazed that I was able to give that light to others while I was going through hell. It's a good and shocking feeling that tells me I was stronger than I knew.

We don't know just how strong we are until we have to be.

CHAPTER 9

My Ticket Out

It's my senior year and I've got a few new friends. Bell is one of them, living with both parents, an older brother and younger sister. She's spoiled and wants her way with her whole family.

Her dad is always quiet, never says much. Every now and then you can catch a slight smile on his face. Her mom is loud and treats me like family. I get yelled at right along with Bell, yet I can tell she still likes me even when she's yelling at me. She laughs and jokes with us all the time.

Her little sister is a momma's girl with a lot of hair. Bell and I fight through that hair. Her brother, Joe, always has jokes. He makes himself laugh and treats me like a little sister. I like to spend my nights there when my dad lets me.

She's got a huge extended family and takes me to a lot of their family functions. They all treat me like family. We run into several of them at O'Dowling. This where a lot of kids in the hood hang out, lift weights, or play basketball.

I am introduced to several hood or gang hangouts through her. It's different. Not what I'm used to but it's coo'. They're all friendly to me. We hang on 13th street by Creative Visions. Police do too.

Anyone who spots the police coming yells, "One time," and everyone runs off. Those don't get away are lined up against the buildings, making them take their shoes off, checking them for drugs. Everyone comes back a little while after the police leave.

Several shootings in the area. A few of our friends are killed. I mentioned someone I knew being killed to my dad and told him I wanted to go to the funeral. He told me I probably shouldn't. I went to the funeral anyway with Bell.

When I got back to my dad's and went to bed, I had a nightmare. Screaming in my sleep. He came running into my room to see what was wrong. I told him I had dream that the dead boy's body fell out of the casket on top of me and I couldn't move.

I felt myself trying to wake up and I couldn't wake myself out my sleep. He said, "You went to that funeral, didn't you?"

Me, "Yes."

Him, "I told you not to go."

I don't know why that one gave me a nightmare. Maybe because he was my age and murdered. I didn't make a big deal out of it though.

Bell's boyfriend lives two blocks over from her. We hang out on his block every time I stay over. That's where his gang hangs and he's one of the leaders it seems. There's guys standing out there all day long every day.

Her boyfriend has a friend who likes me. He's older than me by a few years and I have no clue what to say to this man. Bell keeps trying to coach me, but I'm just too shy.

It's not gonna work. I don't want to talk to him. I usually put my head down or look all around when I'm in front of him, trying not to look him in the eye. He's good lookin', but I don't know how to talk to him or how to act with him.

They take me to my first house party up the street from Bell's house. We don't stay long 'cause some girl from school is trying to fight me, but she's drunk and I don't want to fight. I don't even know why she's coming at me.

Bell's boyfriend, his friend and one of our other friends from school walks us back to Bell's house and the girl follows us. She gets in front of me yelling and screaming about something she says happened in school. I don't know what she's talking about.

I got on my brand new white Ked's and she starts swinging on me.
Oh, not my Ked's.

I can see every swing coming and block them, 'cause I was paying attention when my dad taught me karate. Plus, everybody else is getting in between us.

In the midst of it all I keep looking down at my shoes, worried about getting them dirty. There's a light mist out making the ground a little moist and I don't want my new shoes ruined. With me being so worried about my shoes while she's steady trying to fight me, we fall. She somehow gets behind me and we both slide down off the curb.

Damn it, my shoes!

I jump up real quick, watching her and checking my shoes. Silly to be worried about my shoes in a fight, I know, but I don't like being dirty and It's really not a fight anyway. More of a scuffle. Bell's friends walk us into the house and that's the end of that night.

I tell my dad about the girl trying to fight me and he tells my little sister Natalie. He comes back later and says Natalie wants to fight the girl for me, but I never spoke to Natalie about it.

I was still bothered by the lies my dad said she told on me. My dad had told me a while back that Natalie got in trouble by her mom for dating an older boy and told her mom that I introduced them. That pissed me off.

I've never introduced her to anyone. Her and I have never even hung out, so It bothered me that she tried to put the blame on me, and I didn't want to deal with her.

I'm also back to spending some nights with my mom now that she's getting it together. She's off drugs and doing much better in a two-bedroom apartment with Penny. There's only one bed in the second bedroom, so I sleep on the couch.

She's got a new boyfriend who always wants us out of the way, so he gives me the keys to his car. Penny and I gladly take the car and leave. We pick up my friends and drive all over town driving that car into the ground, literally.

Not much of it left by the time we're finished with it. I tore it up, broke it down. But hey, he gets his alone time with my mom. He complains about the car and still gives us the keys just to get rid of us.

His fault.

I try to go back and forth between my mom's and Bell's on the weekends. This weekend, my dad drops me off at Bell's house on Friday and picks me up Sunday evening. When he comes to pick me up this Sunday night, he's not happy when he gets here.

Bell's mom lets him in and goes to her room while I'm sitting on the couch with Bell. Joe's sitting on the other couch across from us. My dad stands at the door waiting for me to get my things and you can tell he's upset about something.

As soon as we get out the door, he snatches me up and starts yelling at me. He's yelling at me because he swears up and down that I was sitting too close to Joe and that I was only there for Joe.

I'm telling him that Joe was on the other couch and he calls me a liar, keeps saying he saw me with Joe and slams me up against the car. He looks up and sees Bell in the doorway watching so he opens the car door and throws me in. Pissed off, he curses me out all the way home.

He's still yelling at me when we get to the house. Soon as he gets the front door open, he throws me inside and slaps me.

As Denise comes running from the kitchen to see what's going on, he throws me to the floor and kicks me in my stomach.

She grabs him trying to pull him off me, but he pushes her and yells, "Get off me bitch!" He keeps yelling and kicking me and doesn't stop until Denise says she called the police.

They get here quick. When they come in, I tell them I want to go live with my mom, and they tell my dad he has to let me go 'cause I'm old enough to make that decision.

I ask the officer to take me 'cause I don't wanna get in the car with my dad.

I don't want them to leave me with him, but since my dad says he'll take me, the officer refuses and tells me I have to ride with my dad.

Starting to believe my dad more and more, they don't listen to the kids.

He takes me but doesn't let me take anything with me.

I don't care, just wanna leave.

He tries to apologize for hitting me on the drive to my mom because now he doesn't want me to go.

He explains that he got upset and jealous when he saw Joe, the thought of Joe touching me made him lose it.

I don't care. I'm over it.

I finally got my ticket out.

CHAPTER 10

Lost Girl

My mom and Penny moved again to another two-bedroom apartment. Mom's looking better, still with the same guy whose car we destroyed, and money is flowing, so me arriving empty handed isn't an issue.

She welcomes me in with no problem and without asking too many questions about what happened to make me leave my dad's after wanting so bad to move in with him.

Since she didn't seem to be worried, I didn't tell. I spend most nights on the couch because Penny just has a little daybed that's too small for two. They both seem happy with me moving in and I'm more than happy to be away from my dad. Never want to go back there, not even to visit.

I've got a lot more freedom at my mom's now as a senior in high school. Her boyfriend still doesn't care to have us around much. He's sitting in the living room watching TV and we start bugging him 'cause we wanna watch something else.

He gets mad at us for annoying him and calls us some "little bitches."

Ah nah, I ain't going for that so I jump on him and Penny jumps in to help me. When my mom hears her lamp crash on the floor, she yells at Penny and me.

"What the fuck are y'all doing?" so I tell her he called us bitches and she still gets mad and yells at me and Penny. Tells us to shut the fuck up.

I don't like that.

That relationship doesn't last much longer though. Goodbye!

Mom keeps it movin' though. She hangs out late most nights. Some nights she comes in waking me from the couch and sending me to Penny's room because she needs the living room for business.

She also dumps her money in one of my drawers at the end of the night or hands it to me to do so. I feel like her little banker. Keeping count of the money and taking my cut without telling her.

I don't feel bad 'cause It's not like she's working hard at a real 9-5 and I need clothes. I moved back with nothing. Starting over, I gotta go shopping.

I still go to Connie's on weekends sometimes. It's been a minute though and now she's moved and has a male roommate, Bobby. He's like her brother, a little older than me, out of school and more mature.

Come to find out, he's in the same gang as Bell's boyfriend and hangs out on that block too. He takes me riding with him sometimes and talks to me. Picks me up from school one day and starts asking questions. Wants to know where I've been, where I come from, why he hasn't seen me before.

I tell him I had been living with my dad, but now I stay with my mom and don't want to go back. That response isn't good enough. He already knows my mom pretty well and of course hasn't seen me over there, so he wants to know why after all this time I left my dad's and don't want to go back.

He won't let up with the questions, so I break and tell him why without going into full detail. He gets mad and immediately drives me to my mom's. I wasn't expecting this at all.

When we get there, he takes her back to her room to ask her if she knew. He comes back out of the room and tells me she wants to talk to me. When I walk in her room, she's sitting on her bed up by her headboard and tells me to sit down.

I sit at the foot of her bed with my back to her. She asks, "Is there something you need to tell me?"

No response.

"Did your dad do something to you?"

Well when I turn around to look her in the eye, she's smiling, so I say, "No," get up and walk out the room. Her smile hurt. I don't want to talk to her about it 'cause I don't see anything funny and don't understand her smile. It's like she took it as a joke.

"What the fuck is so funny?" It pissed me off. Nah, I can't talk to my mom about shit 'cause she thinks it's a joke. That's damn sure what her expression said to me. Don't wanna talk to her or Bobby about it. Just let it go!

Spending so much time at Connie's, Bobby and I get closer. We talk a lot about whatever. We're sitting in the car right outside her apartment window and he starts kissing me without seeing her looking out the window.

She gets so mad at him for going there with me. She curses him out, but we keep on hanging out. Eventually we start having sex. At least until I find out I'm not the only one he's doing these things with.

I don't know a whole lot about how these situations are supposed to work but I'm sure you're only supposed to mess with one at a time.

His girl approaches me respectfully because she's heard about me. My feelings are hurt so I stop hanging out with him, then Connie tells me about a close friend of ours that he's been seeing.

That's why she was so upset about it. Even though I don't want to mess around with him anymore we still remain friends because he's still someone I can talk to. He believed me when I told him about my dad and acted upset and immediately responded.

Nothing happened to my dad from it and I'm still hurting but he responded on my behalf. My mom, Connie and my cousin didn't seem to care. He asks questions and listens to me.

Connie and Ruby introduce me to alcohol and the club, bringing me in with Cisco and Mad Dog. Oh boy, I'm drunk! Getting in the club with Ruby's ID when the bouncers know damn well it's not me on that ID 'cause they know her well but let me in anyway.

I like the drunk feeling, forgetting about everything else for now so I keep drinking and clubbing. I don't drink everyday but when I do I'm drinking heavily. Drinking, dancing and laughing. It numbs me.

I just want to get drunk and forget about everything for a minute. To me, it's helping. I don't have a care in the world when I'm drinking and dancing. It's like being in my own world, feeling free on that dance floor.

I get up on the speaker in the club and dance not thinking about anybody else in the room. Not caring who's watching. I'm here to forget right now.

I'm hittin' the mall with mom's money for a new outfit every weekend for the club. Now that I've been introduced to these other things in the world, school… well I don't know. I still continue to go.

I really don't want to be here, but I know I have to finish and get my diploma for whatever reason.

Then I try smoking weed with friends. They make fun of how I hold the joint or blunt, saying I look funny smoking. It's really not my thing anyway. I don't like it or see the point of it, but I keep it up anyway 'cause it's the thing to do.

Just like cursing, they make fun of me when I curse, saying I don't sound right doing that either. They laugh at me. I'm a little nerd. I don't know who I'm supposed to be or what I'm supposed to be doing or how I'm supposed to act. I just do shit. Just because! Just trying to cover up my shame.

My mom gets a new man who sales weed and gives it to me to do the same, so now I'm really smoking. I'm in the school restroom with some girls who are talking about getting high off weed, so I'm like coo. I got this.

I say, "I do weed!"

My dumb ass. They fall out laughing. One of the girls gives me a real stank look. I must've sounded real dumb trying to be coo'. Well I tried. She don't even know me.

Another girl put her arm around me laughing and pinched my cheek saying, "She's so cute though." The ugly girl just gave me another stank look.

Start spending time in 'in school suspension.' Go to class one day after lunch with a cup. The teacher tells me I can't have a drink in class and I need to hand it to her. Well, I'm not doing that cause it's alcohol.

"You can't have my drink." She tells me to go to ISS. I let them know that I'm so tired of these four walls, I leave and tell them to let me know when I can come back to class. Drink my drink as I walk out the building. I'm not listening to these people no more.

My mom's new man starts letting me drive his cars. Now I got the weed and the cars. With all this clubbing, different cars and selling weed, it puts me out there meeting more and more men and I start having sex with guys because it's what they want, and this is what you do.

When I say I don't want to, they persist? They won't just walk away and If it looks like a situation that's gonna be hard to get out of, I give in to get it over with. I'll play the role for the moment. Grin and bear it. It means nothing to me. I don't have any feelings. I'm numb to it.

My dad said, "God says there's nothing wrong when it comes to sex," and I keep hearing that even though I'm irritated by the dude in front of me and don't want to do it, but I don't let any of that show. I just do it.

Sometimes it's like I'm really not there at all. Going through the motions.

I keep thinking to myself, *"What if he hadn't done this to me?*
What if?
What if?
WHAT IF!"

I'm a fighter, but in these moments I can't fight. I freeze up feeling like that little girl with my dad. I have no defense. Scared and want the easy way out, I go along with it, but they don't see it.

In their eyes, I'm willing because I can't stand strong on my 'No.' Because I grin and bear it.

I'm starting to feel like sex is what I'm here for. They all want it. It's all they want, so I become good at it.

This is what they want, I'll give it to them.

I smile and play the game because I don't want the confrontation. When it's over I just want to get away from them. I get chlamydia, but I don't wanna have that talk with the guy.

I'm afraid of the confrontation and I'm sure he's just gonna blame me, say I got it from someone else. I'd just rather not deal with him again, so I take my meds and keep it moving.

My doctor tries to scare me by telling me the STD puts me at risk of never having kids. I don't want the STD again, but I don't want kids either. The guys I do get away from call me a tease or a stuck up bitch. I'll take that! If that's the worst of it, HA I'll take that! You're just mad cause I got away from you but I'd be mad at myself for giving in to you.

I get into it with my mom's man because he's always calling Penny "Stupid," and I don't like that. Now that was my curse word when I was younger, so I don't like that.

She laughs, I tell her it's not funny. "Don't let him call you that." I'm always defending her when it comes to him talking crazy to her. I tell him he's the stupid one.

"The stupid ass nigga that can't stay off drugs and out of prison. Don't talk to my sister like that." My mom always defends him and tells me to "shut the fuck up."

I tell her he's calling Penny stupid, but she doesn't care. He says it right in front of my mom, but I get told to shut the fuck up and go somewhere. So one day I do. Sick of her always defending her men over us.

I leave for a few days, wandering the streets. Don't wanna go home, but nowhere in particular to go, so I end up at some friend's house. They're two brothers who hide me upstairs for a couple days. Sneaking food up and having sex with me until their mom comes up and finds me one day while they're at school.

I should've been at school, but I didn't have clean clothes to change into and didn't want to be around anyone.

She makes me leave so I walk the streets until I find someone else to stay with.

It's only for one night because I don't wanna have to have sex with him again.

When I leave there, I go to the pastor's house. My dad's pastor. I want to talk to him and his wife 'cause I just want help. Tired of feeling alone in this. He and his wife welcome me in to sit with them while they sit together on the couch and I sit across from them.

I try telling them what my dad did to me, but it's hard to get out. Soon as I utter the first word, I lose it. I can't stop crying. I can't give detail, but I tell them he had sex with me.

The wife seems upset and the pastor seems disappointed. They both hug me as I'm leaving. After that, I go back to my mom's, who doesn't seem to care that I was gone for a few days without calling. Just another day and nothing came out of telling the pastor and his wife what my dad had done. He wasn't dealt with and I don't feel any better.

Back into routine, driving whatever car my mom's boyfriend gives me the keys to, giving me weed to get off for him. Some nights he lets me keep what's left and I share it with friends.

Then he disappears for a few days and he's definitely missed. My mom's not happy that he hasn't come home or called. He ran off and came back after a few days acting weird.

Running around the apartment in his boxers. Eyes bugged out his head. Sores on the bottom of his feet. My mom said she's not messin with him again until he goes to the doctor.

The funny thing is, he's the coolest out of her friends. He's the only one to talk and laugh with us even though we argue sometimes. He does things for us, even though it's not done right, and I sometimes want to hit him in his head for talking crazy to my sister.

One of the cars he lets me drive is like The Flintstones car. White Cadillac with a blue ragtop. On the outside, it was a nice car. Looks real good. The brakes are going out and a piece of the floor is missing on the driver's side.

It has a metal plate on the floor and if you move the plate, you'll see the ground, but I don't care 'cause I'm rollin' and from the outside it looks real good and others think I got it goin on in here. I don't.

Sometimes I have to honk through the intersection cause the car won't stop. I just hope everybody can see or hear me coming and stop because I can't stop. I run into the back of a friend's car heading to an afterhours one night while I'm drunk and can't stop laughing.

Pushing the brake pedal to the ground and it won't stop.

I keep honking and yelling out the window to warn her I can't stop, but she can't go because of the cars stopped in front of her. There's no damage to either vehicle, so it's fine.

Then I run into a cylinder posted in front of a gas pump and the engine cuts off. Again, I sit there laughing. The guy in the car with me and my friend curses us both out for laughing. We're high as hell. Everything's funny to me. No accident reports. No police interaction. We're safe.

Quit whining.

Then I get the police following me sometimes when I'm driving this car hoping to catch my mom or her boyfriend in it. Hoping to catch 'em slippin'.

They pull me over and ask if my mom's boyfriend is in the car. Then they follow me to the gas station and ask if I want to come work out with them. Nah! Not falling for that. I get pulled over again.

I get pulled over often no matter what I'm driving 'cause they say I don't look old enough to be driving, so it's no big deal to me. So, this time when I ask the officer why he's pulling me over he says it's because I looked like I was about to run the red light even though I came to a complete stop at the red light.

How you gone say I looked like I was about to when I didn't. Come on now! Bullshit!

105

I was about to run it though, until I saw him in my rearview. I was following somebody and didn't want to lose him. I was trying to sale a bag.

Before he approached my window, I told my friend to take the weed out my purse and hide it just in case. She misses one little baggy and the officer finds it when he searches my purse.

He looks at me for a minute and my big cleavage then tells me to dump it out in the grass and he'll let me go.

Alright! I'll take that pass. It ain't that serious. I dump it and head to the club. I appreciate that pass. He could've taken me to jail or found the rest, but he didn't really search. I got lucky.

Thank you, kind sir,

We take off to Fort Dodge for a family weekend. I don't know what I did, but I piss my Aunt Jackie off. I'm sitting at the dining room table with family running off at the mouth. I done got too slick at the mouth and she grabs a belt and tells me to get up.

When I tell her no, she swings at me and I grab the belt. I tell her she's not whoopin' me.

She says, "Oh you think you grown,"

"Uh yea." *I'm doin grown up shit now.*

She asks me if I want to go outside and fight her in the street.

"Yep!" Told her I wasn't gettin no more whoopin's. Tired of folks hittin' on me and I'm so serious.

My uncle's sittin' there laughin', thinking I won't go outside. When he sees me get up to go, he gets up and stops us. I'm so done with the whoopins. You hit me and I'm hitting you back.

I've never thought of disrespecting my aunt because she's always been here for us, but at this point I'm done being hit on. Sick of that shit. I'm damn near grown. I feel bad, but at the same time I couldn't accept that. Just happy the weekend is over once we get back home. I know Aunt Jackie's gonna be mad at me for a minute.

Back at home while hanging out on 21st street; I met Shell from Chicago.

Another spot in the hood. Hanging out there, a few people approach me and tell me I don't fit in. I stand out on the block. I don't belong there, but I hang out anyway and the fact that they're a gang doesn't bother me.

Nobody pushes me away.

They're all coo' with me. So coo, I start going to some of their meetings. I don't speak even though some of what I see really don't like and feel bad for some of those girls. Watching them get jumped on and having things taken away from them is hard to see and do nothing, but I keep quiet. From the looks on some of the other girls faces, I'm not the only one feeling bad for these girls.

I just hang around waiting for them to finish so we can go hang out or stick around for the cookouts. It's like hanging with family.

Shell and I became good friends quick even though she's a few years older than me and has two kids, a little boy and girl. They're like two and three. She also becomes my hair stylist, doing my hair at her house before we hit the club together.

She knows how dangerous the lac is and rolls with me. Calls me crazy. My mom gets us a safer car. Little blue Mercury Lynx. It gets us there.

Racing through downtown in the winter after the club with the fellas. Shell gets scared sometimes so I stop. I was trippin.

This is around the time I see my first dead body on the street. Broad daylight across the street from the bar. Then another on a separate day in front of the same bar. I didn't see either one happen, but I was close enough to get to the bodies by foot before the police got there to close off the scene.

Hard to describe the feeling. I'm kind of numb even at this moment. I can't feel anything for the person that used to be. I want to see them up close.

With one, I walk right up on him hanging out the car door. I want to see his face and the still body. It's interesting. Maybe I can be a Crime Scene Investigator.

Then I meet Rome at a house party. A handsome guy I've seen around town a few times who appeared safe so I left the party with him. Told him I wanted to drive.

I was knowingly speeding when we got pulled over. Rome is over there nervous as hell. The officer comes up and I already know why I was pulled over.

He asks for my license. When he comes back, he says my license is suspended. I already knew that for unpaid tickets. More speeding tickets. Now Rome is looking at me scared as hell.

I play slow, "Oh my goodness. Noo I didn't know. What do I do?"

He told me where to go to find out what I needed to do and let me go. Rome and I continue on with our night and the next time I see him I pretend not to see him. I look the other way because I don't want to hang out again.

I'm not looking for a relationship or anything at all. It's a little awkward trying to ignore him over there smiling and waving at me from across the street while I'm talking to a mutual friend.

I just keep talking to the person in front of me while Rome walks over to talk to me anyway. He wants to hang out again and that night wasn't bad so I go along with it. He turns out to be okay, but I stay guarded.

He asks to see my body one morning after staying the night with him, but I won't let him. I don't want him staring and judging me. I always have something on while walking around him. I'm always covering up, ashamed of my body.

Aside from that, we're having fun together. Getting to be like best friends. Nestled up together during the flood of '93, there isn't a whole lot to do. With no running water you don't really want to do too much running around.

We're boiling bottled water to wash in. Stuck inside with one another, we become even closer.

Once things get back to normal, I start feeling sick to my stomach. My stomach's hurting and I can't eat, feeling nauseated, so I go to the doctor.

He comes into the exam room asking questions and takes a urine sample then leaves the room. I'm sitting here so nervous. My legs are literally shaking when the doctor walks back in with a little bag of goodies and tells me I'm pregnant.

I just lost my damn knees!

CHAPTER 11

Mommy to Be

I said before that I don't want kids and I meant it. I don't even like kids aside from Nya and don't want that responsibility. Ever!

It's too much to be responsible for a whole other life. I'm nervous as hell when I go home to tell my mom; *thinking she's gonna snap on me for this one.*

To my surprise, she's happy as hell.

Wow! I can't believe this.

She's jumping on the phone to tell her friends and so excited that when Rome calls, she answers, "Hi Daddy." I'm looking at her like *"No." Can I be the one to tell him?*

When she hands me the phone I tell him we need to talk in person. Afraid of his reaction, he surprises me with a long tight hug. He's happy and I'm scared at the thought of me being responsible for another life!

Someone depending on me for everything including protection and this is the day I'm supposed to be initiated into the gang.

Rome tells me I better not. I go to the meeting anyway and when asked if anyone wants out before they get it started, I speak up and they let me leave. Rome's right, I don't want to raise my baby in a gang. I've seen how they treat mothers.

They don't care that you have to feed your baby, they want your money anyway. They want you to do what they want you to do, when and how they want it done. No if's, and's or but's. I got somebody else to think about now. A part of me.

Thinking about this someone else, I have no way to support a child nor myself while pregnant. I haven't had to work because my parents and the hustle supported me. Now I need prenatal care and I can't continue like I have. I was on my dad's insurance for a while, but not now. That ended with retirement, so my mom tells me I need to get on Medicaid.

I don't want to do that because I always hear people make fun of other people on Medicaid. People getting assistance are looked down on. I don't have a lot of options though without a job offering benefits. She says they'll help me and my baby, so I do it.
Not too long after I got pregnant,

Penny gets pregnant and my mom decides we need more space. We move to a three-bedroom house, so we all have our own room with her new man and Rome staying with us.

My mom's not thrilled about Rome staying and it shows, but since he's now my baby daddy she lets him stay anyway. We definitely have a full house again. Running off pregnant emotions Penny and I get into a fight, much like when we were younger except now we have these huge bellies in the way and no wind to be fighting.

All we can do is hold each other's hair huffin and puffin. "You let go." "No you let go." Rome and my mom laugh while breaking it up. Fighting over food.

This good laugh gives mom a little normalcy in the midst of her crazy life. It's big to be a woman here making so much money in the streets. Some call her 'Ma Dukes,' although everybody knows her real name, including the police.

She's well known for what she does and when somebody breaks in and steals her stash from the enclosed front porch, she blames me for not locking the door to the porch.

I'm not the dope keeper, so hey, whatever! She shows them where it is when they come to buy and that's obvious. Nothing was broken, so it's clear they knew exactly where to go for what they wanted. Nothing out of place. In and out quietly. The next visitors made their presence known.

Rome and I are driving to Blockbuster one night to return some movies when I see flashing lights behind me. I pull over and give them my license. They go easy on us when they see my belly and tell us we need to get back to my mom's.

They follow us back.

There's several police cars already there when we get back. They tore my mom's house apart. They don't find what they want on her, but they find something balled up in a men's sock in my room. Something I didn't know was there 'cause Rome didn't tell me and now I'm a little irritated with him.

The police have us sitting on the couch, questioning whose room it is, so I tell them it's my room. Now they're asking me about the stuff and I'm just like "Damn!" I don't want to talk to these people. He could've told me he brought something into the house. Now my mom's mad. They would've had nothing if it weren't for that.

I'm telling them I don't know what they're talking about, but they don't want me anyway. They want my mom so bad they want me to put it on her. I can tell by their questioning.

I don't tell them what they wanna hear so they handcuff me and take me down to the jail with my mom right behind me to post my bond.

It doesn't take long for them to come in and tell me my bond's been posted. I didn't even have time to put on the orange. The house is a hot mess when we get back. In the days after, leading up to court, my mom and Rome are talking to me about the court date and what I should say.

Rome, of course, wants me to say it was mine. He's already been in trouble with the law so he's afraid to get time. He says they'll go easy on me because I haven't been in trouble before, so I take it and now I have a record.

My mom's lost all respect for him because he wouldn't man up and take his own charge. Because he was just fine with putting it on me. I went ahead and did it even though I really didn't want to. Did it anyway to spare my new baby daddy from having to do time, and so he can be here with our baby.

The landlord puts us out after the raid and my mom sends me back to my dad's until she can find another place knowing I don't want to go back. Knowing why I don't want to go back! I'm not happy with her for this one.

I ask Rome if he has somewhere we both can go, and he has nothing. He goes to his brother's and I have to go sleep on my dad's couch. I sleep on the couch because Natalie's in the room I used to sleep in and I don't want to get comfortable here. Not like I really could anyway.

It feels horrible being back in the house with him and even with Denise. She doesn't want me there either. Still the same ol dreadful, miserable ass house, feels like everybody's tiptoeing around each other or me. I hate it here. I hate that my mom made me come back here.

I'm so mad at her and Rome right now, but I keep in touch with my mom daily. I need to know as soon as she finds another place so I can get out of here.

I go out and get my first job at a fast-food restaurant to start getting prepared for the baby. My dad gives me rides back and forth to work. My job is to prepare orders, so I'm at work and the phone rings. It's ringing for a minute. I looked around at everybody walking by like they don't hear this damn phone.

Aye, that's gettin' on my nerves.

I don't have a lot of patience at this point, so I answer it.

"Hello?"

The manager gets mad. Well I'm already mad at her ass. I'm like, "Damn. You don't hear that damn phone ringin'?" I had to answer it. Hell! I can't take that, so she fires me. It's coo'.

I call for my ride and ask for my last discounted meal, sit down in the lobby and eat my food while waiting for my ride. That was a real short first gig. Lasted about a month. I got enough money to get a few things I needed for my baby though. Got my car seat and stroller. Few other small things. It's a start.

My mom found a new place. It's small, real small.

A tiny one bedroom with the kitchen sittin in the living room. I traded one couch for another and I have to share this couch with Penny. Two pregnant girls sleepin' on the same couch and it's not a pull out. If it was a pullout, pulling it out would have us sleeping in the kitchen. Right next to the stove. I don't care though. It's still better than being at my dad's. I'll take it.

A group of us go out to eat one night, Connie and a couple of her friends included. We take up a couple big tables. We're all eating and talking when one of my cousin's friends asks me to get a room with him. I say no.

He obviously doesn't care about the big belly bump. He just wants some ass and gets mad when I reject him, calls my baby a "ghetto bastard." I snap on his trifflin' ass.

No, he didn't come for my child just because I don't wanna screw him! He done lost his damn mind!

I start in on him and the whole restaurant gets quiet. My uncle's shushing me. One of my cousins slides up under the table trying to hide 'cause he's embarrassed. Another one gets up and walks out.

You can hear forks being laid on the plates from other folks in the restaurant. I don't care. "I will beatcho ass."

Then I look over at the other table and Connie's going off on the other friend. I don't know what got her started, but she was going in on his head.

They all get up and go outside. It takes me a minute to calm down and get up. I got a little more to say to this dude. When I finally get up and go outside, I see the other guy pointing a gun in my sister's face.

"You bitch ass nigga. How the fuck you gon pull a gun on a female cause she's talking about yo nappy ass head?"

I go and stand between Connie and the gun and tell this bitch to put that gun down and fight me. I'm not thinking about a bullet in my head right now. I see a gun pointed at my sister and I react.

He doesn't put the gun down until my uncle steps up and tells him to. I'm mad that my cousin won't shut his boy down and then remains friends with him after that.

My cousins and uncle are all calm and peaceful while I'm trippin' 'cause he really pulled a gun on my sister and she's scared. When we get away from all that, my sister and her friends are still shaken.

They can't believe I stood up to the guy. I didn't know fear when I thought my sister's life was in danger nor did I think about my child in my belly. I might be wrong for that, but that's my sister and I reacted! Flight or fight? I'm ready to fight for mine.

A few months later on an early morning, my water breaks on the little couch at my mom's. Since I don't have any contractions, my mom doesn't take me to the hospital right away. Says we got time.

She's not trying to rush to the hospital to sit up there all day waiting. We go to the hospital about six hours later. The contractions just aren't coming, and they don't want to risk a dry labor, so they give me something when I get to the hospital to induce my labor and it only takes my daughter four hours to arrive after that.

The nurse looks at me holding my daughter and asks what her name is. Well I hadn't thought of one, but Penny did! She had a cute little name picked out for her daughter. Only thing is, her daughter isn't here yet, mine is.

So, I look at Penny, smile and tell the nurse that my daughter's name is Shyann. The name Penny had picked out for her baby and she's mad about it. She says, "That's fucked up." I had to though.

I can't think of one on the spot and hadn't been thinking of one throughout the pregnancy. It's okay though, because I'm right beside her when she has her baby.

When the nurse asks for the name of her baby, Penny looks at me and says, "Well?"

I named her baby Camille.

Now this little one bedroom is cramped for real. We just added two more to this place and no room for four on the couch.

So!

My mom makes me go back to my dad's again. This time I tell Rome what my dad did to me and that I don't want my daughter in that house with him. I'm hoping this'll make him step up and help his daughter and I out, but it doesn't. With this stupid look on his face, he tells me he can't help. He's still at his brother's, so I have to go back again and with my daughter.

I keep her close to me. Even take her to the bathroom with me. Put her in her car seat and carry the whole thing into the bathroom. She can enjoy her sauna while I shower.

My mom calls to tell me she's coming to get me for a few errands and that I have to leave ShyAnn.

Now why? Yes, I have a few appointments but why can't my daughter go with me? Why can't my mom sit in the car or lobby with her? Why is my mom not concerned for my daughter?

121

I don't see why this is and I don't want to leave her, but my mom makes me. Soon as I get back to the house, I rush in to check on my baby.

Natalie's sitting on the couch holding her when I walk in. I take my baby to look her over and just hold her. I can't imagine what I'd do if he touches my baby.

I'm sitting on the couch with her one night and she won't stop crying. I'm upset thinking about being in this house again and she probably feels mommy's bad vibes.

My dad and Denise are in the living room with me watching TV. ShyAnn's laying across my lap on her stomach and my dad asks to hold her.

I tell him, "No she's fine." He says, "She can't breathe."

I say, "She's crying ain't she, she's breathing just fine."

I'm so mad right now. *No, he's not holding my baby. I don't care about them trying to watch no damn TV. I'm sick of hearing her cry too, but I'm pissed about being here. I'd rather keep hearing her cry than see him hold her. He got to hold her in the hospital in front of the nurses, that was enough.*

I'm mad at everybody and I do not want to be here. Y'all ain't touching my baby! I gotta get a job so I can get out of here and do this on my own. Clearly can't rely on anybody else to help us.

I have Thelma watching ShyAnn while I work this little telemarketing job. I go to drop ShyAnn off one morning and Thelma tells me she can't watch her anymore. My baby is too spoiled and cries all day.

A true momma's girl. If she can't see me, she's hollering. I have another friend, Alex, watch her. She does it for a few days and then the same thing. ShyAnn is too damn spoiled. Only wants Mommy. Nobody can calm her down.

My dad gives me rides to drop ShyAnn off and then to work. The morning that Alex says she can't watch her anymore I'm frustrated.

I know my baby's spoiled, so I know they're having a hard time with her. She's spoiled because I keep her close to me. I'm always holding her so they can't hold her and talking to her.

When I get back to the car and tell my dad I have to find another sitter, he says to me," I can watch her, I won't do anything to her." Sigh... "No, I quit!"

Ain't no way in hell he's watching my daughter.

The thought of him changing her diaper, HELL NO! That ain't happening. And the fact that he would even make that comment about not doing anything to her, NO!

I just can't go back to that job. I'll keep my child close to me to protect her.

My mom moves again to a duplex where Penny and I have our own rooms again. My mom gets me a ring for Mother's Day with my birthstone and a car to get me and my baby around.

Being at home with my mom is coo, but I find myself bothered by my mom always wanting to be the one to bathe and feed my baby.

Don't get me wrong, it's great that she wants to participate in her grandchild's life, but I want to do this. This one's mine. I never wanted kids but now that she's here she's everything to me.

I love her so much and I want to be the one to raise her. I don't want the wrong influence on her.

My mommy instincts kicked in immediately. My mom had her chance at motherhood with us, I want to raise my child so I have to move out. I don't want to tell my mom though. I know she'll be bothered, so I don't tell her until I already have a place, kind of on moving day. She's a little upset, but it's time for me to be on my own.

Rome and I get a place together and my mom stops by almost every day to see ShyAnn. Every time she comes to get ShyAnn I get in the car too.

I heard my mom telling a friend of hers that you don't see kids my age (19) wanting to be that involved with their kids. I'm very protective of mine.

Others ask to babysit my daughter because they think she's so cute, but I don't want to let her go. Plus, with my daughter being such a cry baby when I'm not close to her, I don't want anybody to get frustrated and hurt her.

I know my mom and the life she leads, so I'm not letting her take my daughter out without me there to look after her. I'm worried about what could possibly happen while my mom has her out. I can't lose my daughter.

Penny and Connie show up to my place one day to tell me that my mom is in jail. They raided her place a few days ago and found what they were looking for.

I'm upset that I didn't get the news the day she went even though there was nothing I could do. She was going to be gone for a while. When I try to visit her in the county jail, they deny me because of the charge I took for Rome.

After this news, I find out I'm pregnant again. This time I'm on the birth control pill and it doesn't work. The apartment we're in is infested with mice and roaches.

The whole building complains to the landlord, but he doesn't do anything about it. I'm in my bedroom watching TV when mice come out chilling' in the middle of my floor and on my dresser. Lights on and all. Bold! Like they're hangin with me.

I wake up on the sofa pit one morning with a tickle in my panties. I know it can't be Rome cause he's at work. Nope, it's roaches in my underwear. Two of em. They got lost in my bush. Nope, I'm done! That's a little too close to my pocket. Time to go now.

The thought of roaches crawling up inside my pocket leaving babies or getting lost and stuck up there is enough. I leave without a thirty-day notice. Leaving some of my things because I don't want the mice or roaches tagging along.

Penny's roommate wants out of their agreement, so we move in with her splitting the rent. Realizing real quick that he roommate situation isn't the best idea, so Rome and I visit his parents in Omaha on weekends.

His dad comes up with a name for me, Pretty Poison. I wonder how he came up with that one but I don't ask. It sticks with me though. I feel like it fits with the way things unfold around me. I'm sure he came up with it for different reasons because he doesn't know what I've been through. He just sees how his son is with me.

My section 8 voucher comes, and I move into a one bedroom a month before having the new baby. With a big shirt, I was able to hide the pregnancy from the landlord. I was afraid if he knew I was having another, he wouldn't give me the place.

I go into labor in the middle of the night with no way to get to the hospital. Rome and I were having trouble with our vehicles. It's the middle of January and the city's covered in snow.

It's snowing at the moment, so taxis are running really slow. I got nobody to call for a ride except my dad. Goodness I'm tired of having to deal with him.

Him and Denise take us to the hospital and sit in my hospital room with us. It's awkward.

I'm thinking to myself; I don't want them in the room when I give birth.

When the nurse asks who's staying in the room when it's time to push, I don't mention them. They get the hint and go to the waiting room when she says it's time to push.

This is a hard labor. Not hard because of the pain of the contractions. I took the Demerol. It's hard because ShyAnn's spoiled ass won't stop crying.

Like she knows an intruder's coming and Rome can't calm her down for shit. The nurses try calming her down and that ain't working either. It's time for me to push and one of the nurses asks me to hold ShyAnn. I just look at her, man, I wanna slap this nurse.

I hold ShyAnn in one arm and she lays on my chest calmly while I push her little brother out. The nurse puts a mirror down there so I can see my baby come out, but once I start to see things open up, I gotta look away. That's too much.

I don't wanna see all that but I'm so happy when I see I have a baby boy. I cry a little. ShyAnn's not happy 'cause she wants all my attention and knows that ain't happening. The nurse brings Denise and my dad back in the room after he's born, but they don't stay long, and I go home with two babies in diapers.

ShyAnn doesn't turn one for another eleven days. She hasn't even started walking yet 'cause she just wants to be held, so I have her in one arm and the car seat in the other.

CHAPTER 12

I Gotta Go

Now with two kids, ShyAnn and Jamal, things are getting tight.

Penny and her daughter come and stay on my couch for a little while. She's about to have her second child.

Rome and I start fighting, some fights getting physical. We're hitting each other. He gets bothered when Jamal cries calling him a little fag. He favors ShyAnn and I don't understand that because she cries way more than Jamal. I don't get it.

When he gets his car fixed, he drives ShyAnn around to calm her. She likes the sound of the loud beats in his car. We're all in the car driving around on a nice sunny day. Just riding down the street listening to the beats. Enjoying the sites and one sight in particular catches my eye.

This boy is fine as hell. My eyes get stuck. I don't know how it happened. I can't help it. All of a sudden, SCHMACK! Out of nowhere I feel a sting on my cheek.

My baby daddy done slapped the hell outta me for staring at this dude.

He should be watching the road ahead, not me. Instead, he backhands me. The boy is fine. I forgot I was with my baby daddy. At this moment, I guess I can see how it happens with men and I'd probably do the same damn thing if it were him staring at some girl. I can't help but laugh. All because of ShyAnn's little cry baby ass. I'm blaming her.

Trying to break her from all the crying, he closes her in the bedroom one day and tells me to leave her. It's killing me to hear her cry. I wanna run in there and pick her up so bad.

When I reach for the door, he holds me back and all of a sudden, we hear a thump. She fell off the bed and I'm pissed. After I pick her up and make sure she's okay, I lay her on the bed and start yelling at him.

I slap him for letting my baby fall off the bed then I pick her up and hold her. She's okay, but I'm still mad. I know he didn't intend for her to get hurt. He was only trying to break her from being a cry baby yet I'm in my feelings at the moment.

My baby was in there crying for me and he wouldn't let me get to her. It takes a while, but eventually she stops all the constant crying and shares the space with her little brother. The very small space. It's only for a moment. With two kids, we move to a two-bedroom apartment.

Much better!

The kids have more space and the doctor puts me on the Depo this time instead of the pill. I figure I have it just right now, one boy and one girl. No more.

I wanted my tubes tied, but the doctor said I'm too young and two kids is not enough to tie your tubes. He says I have to be twenty-five or have five kids for him to tie my tubes.

Oh no!

Things get a little crazier with Rome and me. Gets to a point where we're both messing around on each other. He's hardly around and I come across someone I can talk to.

We may as well cut it off, so I figured I'll take my key from Rome and end this situation.

After taking my key, I'm sitting on the living room floor with the kids when I hear a key in my door. I turn around and Rome walks in laughing, dangling a key in his hand. He tells me, "You don't know how many copies I made." Ha-ha!

Meanwhile, I'm trying to keep up with my mom and Ruby, who's also in the same prison: writing to both of them. They say the letters help to get them through the time, so I go through the motions with that.

Letting them know what's going on with us outside. Putting money on their books when I can.

My job's alright, but I can't do a whole lot. My kids and I visit as well. Then the prison decides to dig into my background and find the drug charge I had. It's a misdemeanor with a deferred judgment, but they use it to stop open visits with my mom yet they continue the open visits between Ruby and I. The games they play just because they can.

Now we have to visit in a room where a wall and window divide us. She doesn't want me to visit her like that again, so I don't. I just visit Ruby.

Rome and I try to work it out for the kids, plus according to him no other man's gonna want me since I have kids and that we should stay together for them, so I do. In trying to work it out we have sex a lot.

I feel like it's my job and sometimes I make a game out of it. Playing to get reactions out of him or to see how many times I can get him to orgasm back to back. It's what I've been programmed to do and it's on my mind so much. It's what you're supposed to do, so I do.

I even initiate it, it's not always about the sex itself though. Wasn't until after I'd been with him for a little while that I orgasmed. I want security and affection and don't know what other ways to get it. Sex at least brings our bodies close.

That's when he's holding me and I sometimes think it's more of the sex that keeps us together, not the kids.

With ShyAnn and Jamal getting older, it's about time they have their own rooms. A boy and girl shouldn't have to share a bedroom, so we move to a three bedroom. This one has a washer and dryer in the unit.

Whoa, big step up.

No more laundromat or waiting and listening for the washer and dryer in the hallway to be free. No more saving quarters. Even better, no more lugging laundry and kids to the laundromat!

Rome goes to jail after the move and I keep up with his car while he's in there. That's his baby. I make a couple car payments at the Buy Here Pay Here lot so he'll still have it when he comes out. Plus, I need the transportation.

My car is junk, so I can ride around bumping his music for a minute. I have it all washed and shined up for him when he gets out. I also get rid of his work for him while he's in there, but of course when he gets out, it's just more of the same.

My kids are in daycare while I work. He does whatever.

I need a new vehicle now that he's out and my credit is no good. I need a cosigner and no one to call. No one but my dad of course. So, I do.

I get my new Blazer just in time for pregnancy number three. I got pregnant again and on the depo. I'm so mad the day I find out. I go get drunk. I had a boy and a girl, it was perfect and I was done. I don't want anymore. Damn it! I'm doing all I can to care for and protect the two I have.

Connie and Penny are always getting on me about the way I am with my kids. They're always telling me I'm too overprotective. I don't care. I know what can happen and how quick and easy it can happen.

I won't even let them play outside unless I'm out there with them. I don't care if it is just the front or backyard. Anything can happen. I know! People are crazy. And now this miserable pregnancy has got me moody as hell.

They're feeling it on my job. I go to work telling my supervisor what I'm not gonna do. "My back hurts, I'm not doing shit. Get out my face." I've threatened to whoop my supervisor a couple times. I tell them I will tear that bitch up. I don't know why they don't fire me.

I kicked a coworker in the knee for flirting with me at work. I told him to get out my face and he kept on. He left me alone after I kicked him though. Then they end up cutting my hours, so I go to HR for that one.

They noted that they cut my hours due to my pregnancy, but I didn't ask for my hours to be cut nor did I bring in a doctor's note requiring my hours be cut. They end up giving me back my hours.

My Aunt Jackie works for the same company, in a different building. She told Penny that Rome is screwing a girl that works in the same building as her and she didn't want Penny to tell me, *I don't know why! Hmm!*

The kids and I go for a little ride that evening since I don't have a sitter. I'm looking for Rome, but I find the girl instead. She's in the car with a girl I work with in my building, so I pull alongside them with the windows already down and say "Hey!"

She already knows who I am and why I'm speaking to her. You can tell by the look on her face. I ask, "Are you pregnant by Rome?" She says, "Yes." I say, "Come on and get in the car with me, let's take a little ride."

She looks a little nervous, so assure her that it's not her I'm after. I won't fight over a man. She gets in the car and off we go driving around town looking for him. I can't find him, so I go to my Aunt Jackie's and call him. I'm real pleasant on the phone, ask what he's doing, tell him to come by my aunt's for a minute.

I have ole girl come on in and have a seat while we wait for him.

My aunt, uncle, and one of my uncle's friends are there laughing at the whole thing. I don't care, I'm waiting by the door. When I see him pull up, I tell her to stand on the side of the door so she can hear the whole thing, but he can't see her.

When I go outside to question him about her, he claims he doesn't know who she is. I expected the lies. I say, "Judith, come on down." Just like the Price is Right.

When he sees her step out the door, he tries to make a dart for his car door, so I jump in front of the door. "Uh uh. You ain't going nowhere."

He starts boohooing and trying to get away. I slap him and grab him by his collar. I hear somebody yell for my cousin to grab me. She tells them no because I turn psycho.

My uncle and his friend grab me, but I'm not letting go. I'm trying to kick him in his nuts, but my damn stomach's in the way. Seven and a half months pregnant, I can't get my leg up high enough to reach his damn balls. I done tried a few times. Damn it!

They're still holding onto me and I'm still holding onto him. I tell them, "Just let me hit him one more time y'all, let me go."

They're not letting me go so I slap my uncle's friend, "I said let me go."

He still won't let go.

I finally give up and Rome runs off, jumps in his car, and drives off. I really wanted to hurt him. I didn't have anything else to say to the girl after that. I just wanted her there when I confronted him so he couldn't lie. She calls for her ride and leaves. This is a hard one to handle.

We've been together for about six years and for a while we were like best friends. We were almost always together in the beginning talking, laughing, drinking, having a good time, but once things fell off, we couldn't come back. I guess that's what happens once you have kids and you have to grow up.

Sometimes you can get over one cheating, but it's different when there's a child involved. That child is going to be a constant reminder that he cheated on me. Every time I see that child I'll be reminded how the child got here. I can't do it.

Not only that, but he cheated on me raw. Could've brought an STD back to me and my unborn child. It's too much. We get into it about him cheating another day while sitting on my couch. He sits right next to me and acts like he can't hear me.

I can't stand to be ignored. "So you really gonna act like you don't hear me." Schmack!"

I backhanded his ass.

Blood starts running from his nose. He jumps up and stands over me holding me down and lets the blood run down on me.

Oh, I'm mad. With the weight of Rome cheating and having a baby on the way by someone else, my family and what my dad did, I'm suffocating. I can't take it and it doesn't feel like it's gonna get any easier. I just wanna leave town, but I can't leave being so close to having my baby, no money and nowhere to go.

Then I get the news that my dad's in a nursing and rehab facility. His condition is getting worse. Sigh...I don't wanna see him, but I feel like I have to, so I go.

Denise is sitting beside his bed when I get there. I'm standing at the door not really wanting to walk into the room. She gets up and offers to take the kids out to another room while I visit with him.

I walk around to his bedside with my head down. Hesitating to look up at him with no clue what to say. I'm so hurt when I look up and see him. I just wanna cry.

I'm speechless and I'm not hurt because he's hurting. I'm hurt because what he put me through rushed back and now I'm supposed to have some type of sympathy for him. I'm supposed to feel sad for him lying in this bed and I can't, and he knows it.

He's thinking about himself though. He says to me, "God said if you forgive me, he'll ease my pain."

Wow!

The nerve to want my help now. I still can't say anything. When Denise comes back with my kids, I leave.

I keep up with my cousin in Denver and when I tell him what happened with Rome, he suggests I move there. So, I make plans to do so after my baby is born.

I let Connie and Penny know I'm planning to leave, but they don't believe me. Connie did tell me she's glad I changed though. I'm no longer the selfish little bitch she always called me. Hard to be selfish once I became a mom. My kids take all I have.

I'm so ready to have this baby that I start walking through the neighborhood and walk myself right into labor.

Rome meets me at the hospital, and we have another son. Rome names him Raekwon. He named him that because our son was born the day Wu-Tang released their album. I didn't know that. The next day, I'm lying in bed waiting to see my son. The nurse comes back to my room from the nursery empty handed. Says she needs to check my wristband because she's having trouble finding my son.

I'm about to panic. I know ain't nobody took my son. She comes back in with my son checking both our wristbands again. Says she was looking for a black baby.

My son is pale with straight hair. Oh, my goodness, she's playing.

Don't take my son back to that nursery. I got him!

Three babies and I'm loving them even though I never wanted this.

I love them and they love me unconditionally. Everything is about them. I won't be like my parents were. They did teach me how to be a mommy by making me a protector. I don't want my kids to feel any of the pain I felt. I don't want anybody to hurt mine. I'm determined to protect them from all that.

My kids and I drive out to Denver a few months after having Raekwon to find an apartment. I stay with my cousin Twon and his parents. His dad is my dad's brother. His mom and I don't get along at all. She doesn't like me, and I don't like her. I don't know what her problem is with me but I don't like her attitude. I try to be out of the house as much as possible.

I hang out at my other cousin Latrice's place when I'm not out looking for a place to live. This is where I'm introduced to Paul Mason or 'Freaky Mason' as they call it.

I'm sitting on the couch when one of her friends hands me the bottle. I'm drinking while we're all talking and laughing. Somebody asks if I'm okay. "I'm fine." I don't feel anything so I keep drinking. It's all good until I stand up and go straight down. That's when they tell me it's a creeper.

I'm crying real tears. I ain't neva' felt this drunk. "Please help me! Somebody get this off me!" I don't like this feeling at all. I can't even be here for my kids, I'm so drunk. Can't change Raekwon's diaper. I wake up in the middle of the night struggling to change and feed him. One of Latrice's friends gets up to help me with him.

I stay over for a couple days and there's frequent traffic. She enjoys the company of friends. While I'm in her room with the kids including her son, I hear a commotion coming from the living room. Sounds like somebody's fighting.

I walk out with Raekwon in my arms and see Latrice fighting some drunk dude while two other guys sit on the couch watching and everybody else walks out the door.

I go back in the room to put Raekwon down on the bed and tell the other kids to watch him. I close the door when I walk out.

Latrice is on the floor with this dude on top of her, so I pull him off and fling him across the room telling him, "You gon have to get the fuck up off my cousin."

She gets up and we're ready for him to come back. Instead, he gets up and walks out the door. If he wasn't so drunk, we might've had a real fight on our hands. Glad we didn't.

Wanting to show me more of Denver, one of Twon's friends takes me to a club one night while Twon watches my kids. As soon as we walk in the club, I notice people looking at me and I get mad, "What the fuck ya'll looking at!?"

He grabs me quick, "No no no no no, don't do that," he says. Tells me they're just looking because I'm pretty.

Well tell me somethin 'cause I thought they wanted to do something, and I was ready to get it in. I don't like being stared at. Hate it. To me that means you want something. You're sizing me up.

Don't do that!

I done already said eye to eye contact makes me uncomfortable.

It took a few weeks, but I found an apartment. Now, it's back home to pack and they tell me my dad's been moved again, so I have to go see him at this new facility.

I still can't utter up any words to speak to him. He gives me the same look as before and says the same thing about forgiving him.

I keep my visit short and let them know I'm moving to Denver before walking out. I leave for Denver not long after, and call my sisters when I get there to let them know I made it. They're surprised because they didn't think I would really do it.

I Had to get out of there.

CHAPTER *13*

I Forgive

After a long drive with the kids and family friends driving the U-Haul behind me, I arrive in Denver hoping to feel better getting away from it all back home. It's cold, the ground covered in snow, and I'm nervous and anxious pulling up to my new apartment.

Ready to get the keys and get unloaded after driving all night only for the leasing office to tell me they had a mix up and my apartment is not ready.

That's not what I wanna hear.

The man has a solution though. He offers to put me in a two bedroom until my three bedroom is ready, so we cram everything in there. They only anticipate us being there for a month, so we'll live out of boxes for now.

I moved with very little as far as money goes, so we have a lot of mac n cheese nights. The kids don't mind though. To them it's a full course meal and it'll be our Thanksgiving meal.

They're so young they won't know the difference. We're in here chillin' when I hear a knock on my door, It's management bringing us a whole Thanksgiving meal. I didn't ask for it.

I didn't tell them we were strugglin', but I'm grateful and emotional fighting to hold back the tears.

It lasts us a few days and when the three bedrooms' ready, maintenance staff moves all my things from building to building. A big relief because I didn't know how I was going to get it done if they hadn't. Now I can unpack and get comfortable.

There's not much of a view, but I still just sit and look out the window, glad to be away from home. Loving the peace and quiet. After I put the kids to bed, I take my time to unwind. It doesn't take long for me to feel alone out here even with Twon and Latrice out here. Still feels like it's just me and my kids.

I know this won't be easy, but I had to get away. Denver is much bigger than Des Moines and the cost of living is higher. To top it off, ShyAnn and Jamal start asking for their dad, making it even harder. With the distance there's nothing I can do.

It wasn't my intention to take them away from their dad, but I couldn't stay any longer. I try explaining the distance to them, but they can't really understand at two and three.

They're gettin' on my nerves with all the crying. I call Rome from time to time to talk to them and talk about him coming to visit them. They just keep on crying. Irritating!

Now I'm yelling at them cause I'm not going back. They're just gonna have to get used to being without him. They're driving me crazy. Jamal's only crying because ShyAnn is. He doesn't start until she does and I can't take it. We need to get out of this apartment.

We get ready to go run some errands and my truck is gone.

Great!

When I call the police to report it stolen the first thing they ask is if I'm behind on payments. Well of course I am, so I hang up the phone. I don't have a job yet, so I've missed a couple payments. I call my dad's house to ask if they know anything about it.

Well yea they do, Denise told them where I was. Yeah, of course she did! No money, no job and no transportation to look for a job in this big ass place. It seems big to me because I didn't go far back home and here everything is far.

I don't know anything about where I am. No clue about Denver, Colorado. I just wanted to get away from home, my cousin told me this would be a good move for me and so I did. I'm just gonna have to figure it out.

The kids meet a new friend at the apartment complex while they're on the playground.

His mom invites me and the kids up to her apartment where we meet the rest of her family. They're coo', so we hang out for a little while. Before we leave, she invites us to church, and I accept.

The next day we all pile into her station wagon and head to church. While we're there I notice the bald-headed drummer, who's looking at me.

After church, she introduces me to a few of the members, including the drummer and we leave. It wasn't bad, so I keep going to church with her every Sunday.

Thanks to taxes I get a new minivan. It's not much but it works and now I'm able to drive myself to church and look for work and childcare.

Me and the kids get out and explore a little bit of Denver. People stare at me a lot when I'm out with my kids and I get so irritated.

What the fuck are you looking at?

One day a little girl asks me to play with her, so I ask her how old she thinks I am. Well, she thinks I'm thirteen. I tell her I'm 23 and she's gonna have to find somebody else to play with.

That's when I realized why people keep staring when they see me out with three babies.

They're wondering why this little girl is out with these babies. Still don't like to be stared at though.

My neighbor takes me out to the bars and her nieces watch my kids at my place. She introduces me to one of her male friends one night telling him, "I know you'll like her. She's pretty."

I see him again at her apartment and we hang out. When I'm not with her I have my cousins over. We eat, drink, and play games after I put the kids to bed. All keeping my mind occupied. Making a life out here.

My neighbor calls and tells me, Todd, the drummer from church wants my number, so I give her the okay and he calls right away. My self-esteem is so low at this point.

Rome told me I gained weight after having Raekwon so now I'm feeling overweight wearing sizes five to seven and unattractive. I'm more concerned about my kids than myself. Making sure they have all they need. Making sure they're fed, clean, heads done and decent clothes.

So, my clothes aren't the best. My mom was keeping my hair done when I moved back with her from my dad's. I was getting my hair done every two weeks. I'm not able to keep up with that on my own so I'm not feeling too cute at all.

Now here comes Todd and he keeps telling me how beautiful I am in his Barry White voice. How he loves my long black hair and of course my slim waist and big boobs.

When I answer the phone he says, "Hey beautiful." His voice is so deep, and it makes me feel good.

Compliments for a change. Not telling me no one will want me or that I'm overweight. He tells me I make him look good and that he wishes I was his baby momma. He saw my kids at church and thinks I make beautiful babies. I should've run, but I didn't.

After meeting my kids, he went out and got a second job to help us out even though I didn't ask for his help. I even suggested he go find someone else. Someone with no kids because he doesn't have any and I already have three.

I tried to get him to see that he still has a choice. He doesn't have to be tied to this, but he doesn't want to move on. He even put my babysitters out one night, said they were both flirting with him trying to wrestle him in my bed one night when he got to my apartment before I did.

Guess I can't trust them, and I'll never have them babysit again. After that, Todd and I got a little closer. He came one day with a duffle bag to do laundry and it turned into an extended stay.

A couple months after dealing with him I find out I'm pregnant again. Still on the birth control pill, a different pill from the past.

After Jamal, I checked with the doctor to make sure I was taking the pills right. Same time every day. That's what I was doing. Not working out! I really need my tubes tied. I'm not calling home to tell this one 'cause It's nothing to brag about.

When the doctor tells me how far I am, I think to myself, "Oh man. This might not be Todd's baby."

I tell Todd I slept with someone else before him and it's most likely the other guy's baby, but he doesn't care. He wants to tell people the baby's his anyway when it comes, so I leave it alone for now.

Trying to go about my life and still going to church. Listening to the pastor preach. He hits on forgiveness and I decide to forgive my dad. Hoping it'll help me get over this pain and heaviness.

It's November of 1998, a year after I moved to Denver. I'm not gonna call and tell him. I shared it with God and God alone. Then I'm sitting on my couch watching TV one night when I get a call from Penny.

A week after I forgave my dad. She says,
"Guess what!"

I say, "What?"

151

She says, "Your dad just died."

"What?"

She says, "Your dad is dead."

I hang up the phone and she calls right back. "Did you hear what I said?" I tell her to stop lying and then call Denise. It's true. She says he didn't suffer in his last week. He refused his treatments and wasn't in any pain. Smiling in his last week on earth.

I don't even know how to explain what came over me. The kids are asleep. I'm kind of in shock. I slide off the couch onto the floor and just sit staring at nothing. I'm at a loss.

What now!

I can't afford to get there for the funeral, so I called Aunt Jackie to send us bus fare home. A very long bus ride. Straight to the back to be close to the toilet for the kids.

ShyAnn sits next to some older white lady and won't stop talking to her. Keeps calling her grandma. I don't want this lady to get irritated with my daughter so I'm telling her to be quiet and let the lady rest, but the lady insists it's okay.

So ShyAnn continues, "Grandma. Grandma. Grandma."

We go to Connie's as soon as we get home 'cause I don't want to take the kids to the funeral home. Their dad and his new girlfriend pick them up from Connie's.

The girlfriend sees me bring the kids to the door and puts the car in reverse. Backs up a little. I had no intention of going to that car messing with her. He took the kids to the car and they left. I have to go view the body.

I look straight ahead at the coffin when I walk into the funeral home. There's a few people there already. Mostly on the right side of the sanctuary. The Pastor comes walking towards me and I start crying immediately. When he reaches to hug me, I tell him, "I don't even know why I'm crying."

But I can't stop crying. *I thought I should be happy he's dead.*

I walk around the Pastor and Natalie comes up to hug me. My eyes are on his dead body in that coffin. After hugging her, I take a seat on the left side and a couple family members come up and hug me.

I can't stop staring at that coffin crying.

Then I hear others crying and some of his nieces saying he was their favorite Uncle. I hear it again and again. It bugs me. I really don't wanna hear that. I really don't.

Walking into the church the next day for the funeral, again I cannot stop crying. I sit in the front row of the church and drop my head covering my face crying. I don't hear a word spoken at his funeral. We're at the cemetery and I still can't stop crying.

I walk up to the casket for a closer look at him.

Later on, back at their house, Denise asks if I want any of his things to keep. She offers me his Chicago Bears sweatshirt. That was his favorite team and his favorite sweatshirt. He wore it a lot and I wore it a few times. I wore it to school for spirit week.

It still smells like his musk. I don't want it. I look up and see the bottle of his favorite cologne on the dresser. I take that instead.

I don't recall the smell of the cologne on him. I can only recall the smell of his natural musk. The Stetson cologne is in the shape of a gun, and I take my old alarm clock. That's it. I don't want anything else. '

Why I took anything, I don't know!

It doesn't really hit me until I get back to Denver. That's when the anger sets in. I'm angry at God. I forgave him and God let him off the hook. He didn't even suffer in his last week. Lived his last week in peace after I forgave him. I don't feel that's fair.

My words to God, "You let him off easy and You left me here to suffer. Why would you do that? Why couldn't it be me? Why couldn't you take me?

I'm still here.

I still have to deal with this!" I'm so mad. Pissed!

"WHY?"

He's not suffering anymore. I am. It's not fair."

God stayed true and kept His word to him, but how?
How does someone like my dad hear from God and get his prayers answered, but I can't. Not that I prayed about this, but still. I think about God and I do believe in Him, but I don't know how to talk to Him.

Why won't God speak to me? Why him over me?

I have a book called 'How to Hear from God.' I don't remember how I got it, but I guess now's the time to check it out. I'm trying to read this book, but I can't focus or retain any of it.

I think about suicide. I want to do it, but I think about my kids and worry about who's gonna take care of them if I leave. I know nobody will love them or protect them like me.

I know there's nobody in my family that would take them, so they'll be with strangers. Most likely separated so I have to stay to take care of them. I don't want anybody to hurt, mistreat or neglect them, so I have to stay.

Todd and I fight over simple things. I'm tired of his smoking and having to smell it, his lies and him period. I find out from one of his friends that he had sex with another girl while I was at my dad's funeral. He says he did it because he thought I was back home screwing my kids' dad.

Then I start having complications with my pregnancy, having pain in my stomach, and spotting so Todd takes me to the hospital. They check me over and send me home. Tell me I have Chlamydia and gave me a one dose prescription to get rid of it, said it'll be safe for the baby.

I'm feeling even more pain after taking the medicine, feels worse than labor. Got me crying, the pain is so bad. Todd doesn't know what to do, so we're going back to the hospital and It's a real struggle to get dressed. He helps me get dressed and in the car.

All of a sudden, the pain just stops, and it feels like something's coming out. I can feel something sitting right there between my legs and I'm scared to move. I feel like as soon as I open my legs it's coming. I don't know if it's blood or some other fluid, but I keep my legs locked.

They bring out a wheelchair when we pull up to the hospital and I slide out onto the seat of the wheelchair. I'm telling the nurse I gotta pee so she wheels me into the restroom. Her and Todd stay there with me.

I'm so scared to open my legs, but she tells me to go ahead and it'll be ok. Soon as I squat to pee my baby falls in the toilet. I scream and Todd laughs.

The nurse looks at him and rolls her eyes. She assures me it's okay and that they'll get my baby for me, so I get back in the wheelchair scared for my baby.

Once I'm in my room they bring my baby in. A stillborn in a bucket. Still in the sac. He's balled up. Tiny hands and feet.

I was almost six months along and had already felt him moving. Just earlier in the day I felt movement. I'm mad because I was just here, and they sent me home. The doctor assured me the medication wouldn't hurt my baby and everything would be fine.

The next day the nurse brings me some paperwork with his footprints and a stuffed yellow duck. She explains the funeral process for these situations and how they put the babies in a freezer until they get twenty of them. Once they get twenty, they notify all the families and put them all in one coffin for one big funeral.

I told her not to call me. I'm not coming to watch that. I've been crying for days. Then I think to myself, maybe it's best I lost him because of how he was conceived. Now I don't have to worry about whether or not to tell the actual father. That and the fact that I don't need another child anyway.

After that, I start having this nightmare. It's the same damn nightmare over and over and I wake up at the same point every single time.

I have a baseball bat and I hit my dad in both legs, breaking him down to his knees and then as I swing that bat at his head, I wake up crying every single time.

I never get to connect that bat to his head. Not once and it bothers me. Crying after every nightmare. I'm mad that I never get to hit him in the head. Maybe I'll feel a little better if I get to bust his head open and see the blood splatter in my dream, but it never happens.

I have visions of him in the back of a police car and thoughts of him being murdered in prison. I keep it all to myself.

I finally tell Todd what my dad did. Just that he took my virginity. His response, "I wish one of my aunts would have done that to me. I got some fine aunts."

Why is that your response?

That's so inappropriate, and I know now not to talk to him about it anymore. He'll just agitate me.

I begin to smell my dad. Just out of nowhere. Not even thinking about him and all of a sudden I can smell him like he's right here. I know his musty smell.

I look around like he's really here while hoping I don't see him. I hate the smell. I fight back the tears and it puts me in a bad mood. I'm easily irritated and the kids set me off quick. Gets me yelling and whooping their ass with that belt. It's a good leather belt too.

I'm trying to raise them right. Better than how I was raised. Not like my parents, but I'm angry and it causes me to struggle. Trying not to take my anger out on them.

Finding small ways to soothe my mind. Spending hours on jigsaw puzzles. Helps with patience and clearing my mind.

Trying to get a little me time by sending them to their rooms or the quiet after they've gone to bed. I raise them to say yes ma'am and no ma'am. I don't drink in front of them. Teaching them boundaries.

Letting them know that no one is supposed to touch their private parts. I make sure they can wash themselves in the tub in case I'm too busy. I don't want Todd or anyone else bathing them.

Try to ensure we have great communication, want to make sure my kids feel comfortable enough to talk to me about anything. They're young, but to me it's not too early to start. Yet every little thing they do wrong irritates my soul.

Breaking stuff, playing in my hair products, fighting each other. I can't stand them fighting each other. I do not want them like me and my sisters. I want to make sure they show each other love and are always there for each other.

For the most part I think I got it. When it's break time for me, they have no problem going to their rooms to play. But sometimes I get a little leery of the quiet. They get too quiet and I know they're up to no good.

Every time!

Then I just lose it one day and have to call Twon. I beg him to please come get my kids. I need them to get the hell away from me 'cause I can't take it.

Man!

The look in his eyes when he walks through the door. He doesn't know what to think. He's never seen me like this.

I'm on my knees crying.
I need him to get these kids away from me before I really hurt 'em and I don't want that.

161

It's not their fault. Just need a few hours alone.

I reach out to a therapist after that and the first thing he does is pull out a prescription pad. I don't want drugs and I don't pick up the pills or go back to him.

Pills will only mask it.

I need real help and don't get a genuine vibe off him. Feels like he just read books for a check.

I try talking to the pastor's wife out here and that doesn't work either. She says she went through something similar and apparently she's still angry and hurting too. She can't help me heal when she's still there.

CHAPTER 14

Where's God?

We go to church one Sunday morning. Nothing special. Not a lot of people in the pews, so I don't have to sit close to anyone and I don't. No one close by.

The pastor starts his sermon and as he's preaching, he turns to me. Looks right at me, points and says, "God said to tell you He was not there when that happened to you!" Then looks away and moves on with his sermon.

"What the hell?"
"For real?"
"Why... would you say that to me?
Are you serious?
WHY NOT?
"Why was He not there?"
"You're not even gonna explain?"

This does not help me at all. *Now I'm mad because you're telling me God stepped aside to let this happen to me and I say stepped aside because all this time I was told He's always there.*

Now I'm being told He's not. Why not? How was that supposed to help me? Was that supposed to make me feel better in any way at all? Cause it didn't! Now I'm even angrier.

Why would you tell me that and not go further to explain? What am I supposed to do with that? He's always there except in the moment I really needed Him! God told you to tell me that and that alone? Didn't tell you to explain why he wasn't? That's what you're telling me? Why not? Why did He LET that happen to me? How am I supposed to deal with that?

Where do I go from here? I don't know how I'm supposed to take that or who's gonna answer these questions? Now I'm even more lost.

I'm so confused by the pastor's words. Everyone says God is always there but not when my dad took my innocence again and again. I never even thought about it in that way until the pastor pointed me out and said that.

Now I'm confused and not sure what to believe anymore. I don't want to lose faith. I really don't. I gotta have something other than my kids to hold onto. They can't carry my weight. Need something to give me some kind of light.

I was somewhat raised in the church and I do have faith in God. It's not strong with everything that's happened, but it's something. Now I'm shook and not sure what to believe in anymore.

Going to church is just like going through the motions now, each week I'm here but I'm not here. I can't retain anything the pastor's saying. I can't even hear it half the time. There really ain't no point in me being here but for numbers in the congregation. It's going in one ear and out the other.

Now I watch others in the church and question their purpose for being in the building. I see the fakeness in so many of these folks. I don't believe all these people are saved. Kissing up to the pastor and his wife.

I told Todd's sister, "You can tell folks that's really saved. They smell like Jesus." She laughed and told me I was stupid. I laughed too but I was kinda serious.

Some church folk have a certain smell about them. That Jesus cologne. I can believe those folks are real and they can really pray for you. I don't want those other folks praying for me, and not trying to hear anything they have to say.

You look for the old ladies with the church candy. You know what I'm talking about. Big Momma always has her church candy for the kids. Making sure she has a bag full every Sunday.

Everybody loves Big Momma including me, and she loves me. I know she does. I never told her what I went through but we bonded.

I never had a close relationship with either one of my grandmas and Big Momma made it easy to have one with her. Old folks have a lot of wisdom to share and I just like being around her. She's always got jokes too. You can't try to clown her back though, she'll threaten you with a shoe. She's funny and gets on Todd from time to time about behaving. I love it.

He's so full of surprises. I get a bangin on my door one night. Police are looking for him cause apparently he's gotten into a little trouble. I don't know anything about this, and I just got home with my kids.

They ask if they can search my apartment for him and I give them permission 'cause as far as I know, I've got nothing here to hide.

The apartment was dark when I got home, so I didn't think he was here, and I let them search while I wait by the door with my kids.

One officer walks out of my kids' room asking if that's feces on the wall. No, It's my brown hair gel that ShyAnn and Jamal quietly smeared on the wall and that shit ain't easy to clean off. I tried. One of those things they were doing when it got real quiet.

The other officer came from my room where he found the evidence he was looking for. He didn't find Todd hiding in the damn closet though.

After they leave, he comes out the closet with a stupid ass smirk on his face. I wasn't charged with what they found, but I do end up losing my housing. Now we're homeless, so Todd's mom puts us up in his sister's apartment while she's out of town.

That doesn't go well either. She agrees to let us stay while we figure out a more permanent solution. Todd and I start fighting in that apartment.

Of course, I can't put him out of his sister's apartment and I'm in a bind with nowhere to stay with my kids. He tries putting me out though. Then has the nerve to tell me to be quiet when I get upset about it.

Alright! Coo! I grab a case of canned sodas and start throwing them out into the hallway and yelling. He's trying to stop me and we're fightin'!

Fuck you bitch! Nah, I'ma be loud as hell.

Neighbors call the police and I tell them he's trying to put me and my kids out, so they put me and my kids up in a motel they use for women in domestic situations. A dark, trashy motel. Old linens and sunken beds. You can only stay for three days. After that you're on your own.

So, after our three days were up, Todd's mom and a friend of hers come and get us. We have a little sit down. Sort of a counseling session to keep us on a positive note and stop all the fighting.

I let them know I'm angry and trying to work on myself. Tell them what happened with my dad and her friend's response is, "Aww, get over it."

Now I've been dismissed over and over, but this one and the look on her face!

Wow! I wanna slap this bitch.

Her whole better than thou stank ass attitude really hit. She dismissed me like I was just saying some shit looking for a pity party. They sit us down as if they're genuinely trying to help so I speak up to genuinely receive that help.

I'm not looking for pity, I'm looking for a way to heal. I'm trying to get over it or get through it. I don't like her and I don't like living in the dark either. Clearly! That's why I keep reaching out for somebody to help me find a way to get out of it, but I just keep getting dismissed and judged. Told to go somewhere like I ain't shit.

How am I supposed to open up and get help when this is the response I keep getting when I try? Again, I have to hold it in and put on a smile because nobody wants to hear about the shit, so I go back to the

168

apartment with Todd until I can get the money to go back home.

I had to go to the state for a onetime payment to help me move home and Todd goes with us. He doesn't wanna let go. He wants to keep on trying.
I don't have the strength to tell him he can't.

Even though the Pastor told me God wasn't there at that time, I have to believe he's here now. I may not know how to talk to Him or how to see the signs but I have to hold on and keep trying. That and my kids are what keep me going. Giving me the strength to continue smiling through it all as I begin to tell myself,

This too shall pass!

And Lord, I need you.

CHAPTER 15

Pit Stop

Home again and not trying to stay long. Got an apartment shortly after being back and staying with Penny for a minute and Todd gets two jobs.

I find out I'm pregnant again when I go to get my tubes tied. It's so frustrating because I've tried a different birth control after each child trying not to get pregnant again. Todd and I aren't in a good place and I don't want his baby.

Everything is blowing up and I'm having a fit. I go off on him about how I don't want his baby. Telling him, "You probably make ugly babies. I can handle an ugly boy, but I can't handle an ugly girl."

It was mean and I know it. It's not about the look of the baby, I just don't want a baby by him. Don't want to have to be tied to him. He blows off my rant and tells me to stay home while I'm pregnant this time around, so I do.

Then he tells me that I ain't shit when he realizes he can't handle the finances on his own. Now I don't mind going to work, but this was his choice for me to stay home with his child.

170

Right after giving birth to our daughter, he gets upset with me because he's hungry and I forgot my purse at home with the money. *Forgive me for just thinking about giving birth and getting it over with through the pain of labor.* Lesson learned: never lean on a man for shit even when he says he wants you to.

The nurse offered to bring him a patient meal, but he didn't want that. Oh well, I just gave birth. I'm not thinking about feeding his ass.

I got my new baby girl home and I'm loving her cute little face. Her big brother Jamal wants to hold her, so I tell him he has to sit on the couch first. I don't want him to drop her.

He's holding her up in his arms. Maybe his arms got tired because he relaxed his arms to set her on his lap.

I panicked and yelled, "What the hell are you doing?" 'Cause what I saw was him putting my baby on his private part and I lost it. For a minute, I didn't see my son, I saw some boy trying to hurt my daughter.

I had to catch myself before I hurt him 'cause that's not what he was doing. He was my son holding his baby sister and it was innocent. I'm the one with the problem. I need to take a seat and calm myself down. I do.

My mom ends up getting out of prison and moves into the apartment right under me with Layla.

Whenever my mom wants me to come down, she takes her broom and bangs on the ceiling.

That's my call and she'll keep banging until I show up at her door.

She's very impatient. One night I was tired and didn't feel like going, so she got pissed and came up to my door yelling at me. I didn't feel like going down those stairs. I knew it was nothing serious and I was tired. I figure she'll get over it.

She watches my kids every now and then when I step out. I make sure not to leave them too long since she doesn't have a lot of patience with kids. Don't want her getting irritated and mistreating mine.

So, I go to get my kids from her one day and from outside her apartment I hear her arguing with Raekwon. I stand there and listen for a minute. He's telling her to leave him alone or his mommy's gonna whoop her ass.

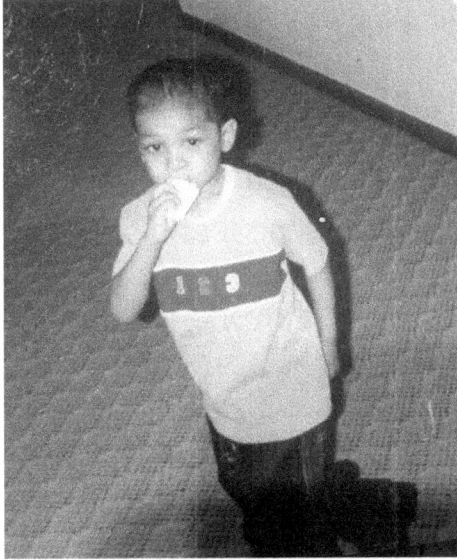

My fault. I told him what to say if anybody messes with him, but I had to ask my mom why she didn't whoop him. Why she's arguing with him because she's got no problem whoopin' ShyAnn and Jamal.

Well they say Raekwon's too much like me and she doesn't like fooling with him.

I didn't stay home for too long. After about a year home, I moved right back to Denver. Being home was still too much for me. I'm not ready.

CHAPTER *16*

Anger Management

On'yai, this last child, became another mama's girl real quick. I like singing to her and playing footsies with her. She follows me everywhere; including the bathroom and screams when I close the shower door even though you can see through it. Soon as I open the door she stops; close it and she screams again.

I step out the shower one night and she asks why my butt is so dirty.

Sometimes I can't stand my own kids. It wasn't my butt she was looking at, damn it! If I could get some damn space. I can't take a dump alone, but it's my fault. I'll take that. Just one of the consequences of being overprotective. They're used to being up under me.

I Love momma's babies. They're spoiled. I turn around after putting a pad on and see her taking the wrapper from the trash to put it in her underwear.

That's when I realize I'm in trouble for real cause she's watching everything I do, wanting to do everything I do, and has to go everywhere I go.

She was with me when I got my haircut. So, when we get home, I find her hiding in her bedroom with some scissors cutting off her ponytails.

Oh my goodness. She ain't got no hair as it is, and I've been working hard to get it growing. Man, I whoop her little ass. Whoop her every time I look at her this evening. Just gotta be copying me.

Anyways, I've been feeling like I might need to further my education to get a better paying job, so I go looking for assistance with that. I can't afford college and I'm tired of the telemarketing jobs I've been getting, they don't last. If you don't make a sale, you're fired.

Somethings gotta give, so I go to a DHS office that can help pay for certain classes. The lady sits me down to ask a few questions about my situation. She pauses for a minute, then asks if I would consider giving my kids up for adoption.

Pause.

It's bad enough that birth control isn't working, now she's trying to make me feel like shit for having my kids.

I don't believe in abortion, so It wasn't an option for me. I laid down and made them so I'll stand up and take care of them. Despite those that say their tax money supports my kids; it takes a whole lot more

175

than money to raise kids and I know four kids is a lot for someone so young and broke. Although my kids don't see that when they look around.

Raekwon tells me we're rich.
I say, "You think so?"
Him, "Yes."

I'm far from rich, but to hear him say that made me feel good and know that I must be doing something right at least in their eyes. To them, they have all they need, and I give them that comfort.

I ask her if she has kids and of course she says no. I didn't think she did because if she did, that question wouldn't have come out her mouth so easy. She clearly doesn't know the bond a mother has with her kids, so I just left.

Found out about another agency that helped me get into medical billing classes. The course is only a few months. I can handle that plus I'm making new friends in the class.

My van brakes down after classes start, so I take the bus, get rides from friends, or use Big Momma's car. I finish the class and receive my certificate. Then end up with a pretty decent job in Medicare and Medicaid lines of business starting out through a temp agency and then on to be a permanent employee with benefits.

Loving the PTO earned every pay period. My daycare is right across the street from me and I take the bus to work. I don't mind. It's only temporary and it feels good to be getting things in order. I have a full-time job, kids are in a good daycare, boys are playing football and the girls are cheerleading.

Things are looking up besides the situation with Todd. Still fighting and It's so petty. He threatens to take back all the gifts he got my kids from under the Christmas tree. When I talk about it being over, he wants to take it out on my kids.

I tell him, "Here, you can have the whole damn Christmas." I pick up the whole tree and throw it at him. The kids ain't got nothing to do with it, but if that's what it takes to get rid of his ass, take it all.

177

We get ta boxing. He got a good one in on my face. I step back, "You hit like a bitch."

With my fist up, I'm going back in. He takes off running out the front door. I'm not done. I'll keep coming and he knows it. He knows the only way to end it is for him to leave. Left a little bruise under my eye. It's alright. I'll keep it pushing. The bruise will fade, and life goes on.

I have a job that's got me feeling good. I'm a customer service rep and every team member has the chance to be the lead for one month. In the lead position you don't have to take calls, you work on projects.

When my turn came around, they asked if I wanted to remain lead and I accepted. I'm in this position for a year before they get rid of it all together. Then it's back to the phones.

Overall, I like the company. I've met some good people here. Some I've become good friends with outside of work. So I walk into my cubicle one morning and my eyes begin to water. It's Thanksgiving time and someone left bags of groceries on my desk.

When I turn around a few of my coworkers are standing behind me and all give me a hug. I gotta go to the restroom to pull it together.

There are some good people out here.

I've moved around in the company a few times. A different supervisor with each position. The first one tried to write me up for something I didn't do when a member called in complaining.

When he brought the write up for me to sign, I told him I would sign it after he checks the notes and brings me proof the mistake was on my part.

There's notes on every call that comes in. A note at least saying which rep answered and took the call and he didn't come back with that paper. I'm not taking the blame. He tried it though. He's gonna have to own his own mistake. He ended up losing his job for several reasons.

My next supervisor always tells me I should quit my day job. She thinks I'm so funny. I think she's too damn happy. Eight AM and she's cheesin. Too damn early for that. She's also the one to tell me I'm pregnant again. I don't know what she sees, but I'm not claiming that. Her and another coworker have me take a pregnancy test in the restroom.

Now this is three years after On'yai, but I'm not trying to deal with another child.

Nope!
I'm not believing it.

I refused to go to the doctor at first. By the time I go I'm three months pregnant.

Fertile as hell!

I was doing so good getting on my feet. So good that my manager came to me one day to tell me she uses me as an example in her meetings. If I can make it to work every day on time with four kids, no excuses, no car, no complaining and do my job, so should everyone else.

It's a nice compliment and had me feeling good that someone noticed my drive and effort.

Thank you!

I saved up enough money to get a new truck while I was riding the bus. Now I can get my kids to practice without bothering other folks.

My sons love playing football for the Pal league and ShyAnn loves cheering for her brothers. That's also the only skirt she's allowed to wear without me around.

Some days she has to ride to another field with her squad. I don't want her wearing a dress or skirt unless she was spending the entire day with me. That means she can't wear them to school. Least, not without shorts underneath.

I need to be able to keep an eye on her. Make sure she's not doing any flips or running around in her dress showing her underwear.

I don't even like her playing tag after football practice with the boys. She's tried and I stopped her. Told her to sit her little fast ass down. Calling her a little floozy. "Ain't got no business running around with them damn boys."

They all practice at the same park but with their different age groups. On game day, they play at different parks and different times.

ShyAnn usually cheers for Jamal. I made sure she's always with one of her brothers to save me from one extra drop or pickup on game day. On'yai practiced with the cheerleaders for a minute, but she quit because they didn't take enough breaks in practice for her to snack. Damn shame! I didn't force her though.

She stays on the sideline with me eating her snacks. That girl loves to eat. After work I get the kids from daycare then to the football practice. From there we go home to cook dinner, take baths, and go to bed. I'm getting it done. I got this mommy thing and I do whatever else needs to be done when anybody else calls, so one more child was cutting into my system.

I feel like I'm doing good with the four I have. Got a good schedule going and doing good keeping them in line. Least I think I am.

Jamal gets in trouble one day in school, so I get the belt out when he gets home. He's seven years old and a little fighter. I got the belt in hand fussing at him and he has the nerve to look me up and down like he's about to whoop my ass.

Ah nah!
He done lost his mutha fuckin mind.

I turn and look behind me to make sure he's not looking at somebody behind me. Nobody's there, so I ask him, "Oh what, you 'bout to whoop my ass? You wanna fight me?"

He's still looking me up and down, so I put the belt down and put my hands up. "What's up!"

I punch him in his jaw, and he falls to the floor hollering. He's not bruised or bleeding, but I bet his ass won't try me again. I had to let him know he don't want none of this and not to ever disrespect me again.

We're good now. Had to show him. I demand their respect. At the same time, I make sure they know I love them. I tell them and show them all the time.

Before giving birth to this one, I take a little break and go home for a visit. My mom hesitates on letting us stay with her because her boyfriend doesn't want us there but lets us stay anyway.

We're only there to sleep and bathe. I don't like her boyfriend and he doesn't like me. I don't like his vibe and It's not that he's into me, but that he's sneaky.

He didn't even want her to watch her grandkids so I can go hang out for one night. We don't live here, so she barely gets to see them. I was gonna be pissed if she said no for him, but she ended up watching them. I can't wait to get back to Denver.

It was a short trip. I'm back at work. Sitting in my cubicle at work, my manager comes over with the classified section. She put her hand on my shoulder being so sweet, she already went through and circled a few jobs for me, saying she's trying to help me out.

Now this is the same manager that was just singing my praises and now trying to push me out the door. I politely take it with no words.

She must not like the fact that I'm pregnant again. Must think I'm gonna start slacking off. Well I took that paper to HR and asked when they became an employment agency. I didn't tell them I was looking for another job. I didn't complain about my hours or position.

Afterwards she was fired, and I applied for another position in the company and got it. Higher pay and a new supervisor.

The pregnancy had me a little moody so she would tell the others in the department that I wasn't at work until ten even though I clocked in at eight. I'm not a morning person. Leave me alone. My previous supervisor still likes to come over and laugh at me. I don't like that she's so chipper first thing in the morning, but I like her.

I start having problems with this pregnancy. He's ready to come out now, but I'm only about five and a half months in.

The doctor was able to stop the contractions and it happened two more times. The third time the doctor put me on bedrest and steroids.

Thanks to FMLA I still have money coming in. He told me I had to stay in the hospital for two weeks.

Todd's cousin kept my kids while I was in there. Even though I know she doesn't mind and I'm comfortable with her, I still feel the need to be home with my kids.

I convinced the doctor to let me out after a week with the order to go home and stay in bed. That's hard to do with the kids. Still need to get them around, plus when anybody else calls needing my help, I'm there.

Big Momma says the devil's trying to take my son and God's gonna sit me down cause I'm doing too much. I don't know how to tell people no. I just keep going and going.

I have a dream that I'm at a four-way stop. After a complete stop, I proceed to go through the stop sign when a car comes flying through and hits me on my driver side.

Not long after the dream, my kids and I are at a red light at a three-way stop. Light's been red for a minute. When the light turns green, I proceed to make a left turn and I get hit.

A little Audi slams into both driver side doors. The lady in the car said she was on her phone and didn't see the red light. She felt so bad when she saw the kids get out and then me, climbing out the passenger side with the big belly at thirty-six weeks pregnant.

We're all okay, but Big Momma was right. That accident gave me a little anxiety and then we get snowed in. He definitely sat me down. Sat me down for a minute. I was not anxious to get back in traffic.

My son came a few days later. The doctor induced me because of swelling in my legs. A healthy baby boy who of course will be spoiled just like the rest. He put my body through it trying to come out early but he's so worth it all.

Because of pain in my neck and back from the car accident, I'm going through routine physical therapy, massage, and chiro. Keeping the smaller kids in daycare and volunteering at the kids' school just to be doing a little something.

I held ShyAnn back in first grade because she struggled, so she was in class with Jamal. I like having them together to look out for each other.

When I volunteer, their classmates are excited to see me walk in the classroom. They often ask to go home with me. One little girl told me she wished I was her mom. Aww! Made my day.

I go on a field trip with the class to the city garden. They're chasing bugs, playing in the dirt, and smelling the flowers. A few kids follow me and another volunteer who came with me to find a spot to sit and rest.

As they stand around us talking and playing, one approaches me with the Froggy voice from the Little Rascal's. He asks, "What's that?" putting his little nasty finger on the mole right above my lip.

OMG.

I jump up screaming. "Why would you touch my lip?"

Gross.

Him, the other kids, and the other volunteer are laughing so hard it makes me laugh. Despite his dirty little finger on my lip it's still a great moment. Seeing those kids laughing and having a good time brings me joy. I love it. They keep me going.

Even the teachable moments like when Jamal comes home from school with his shirt balled up in his arm and a little blood on it.

I ask what happened and he says he was picking on a little girl and when she told him to stop, he didn't. Her big brother came up and punched him in the nose and I can't even be mad about that. The little boy did right protecting his little sister.

Hopefully, my son learned a little something from this. I certainly got on him about hitting on girls and so did her big brother. I'm sure he learned his lesson.

Their elementary years weren't so bad, and I know because I was there close up for much of it. The kids had plenty of friends in the neighborhood and played well with their peers.

Raekwon and Jamal would often go play baseball with the neighbors. The parents would go on and on about how good the boys were at the sport. I love how well my kids get along with all races, including the parents of their friends.

Fifth grade continuation was a big deal for the students. Time to move onto the next chapter. I sat in the second row as the teacher called up each student to get their certificate. It's just fifth grade though. Still have a long way to go so it's really not a huge deal, right!

Well...when the teacher calls up ShyAnn and Jamal, he has a whole speech. I'm surprised. He goes on about how much of a pleasure it was to get to know them. That's not unusual to say about each kid in trying to make them and their parents feel proud.

He keeps going on and then starts crying while he's speaking on how he's going to miss my kids. He makes me cry.

I cry because I raised those kids that touched someone's heart so early in that way and I look over to see their other teacher crying as well. Momma's babies.

While I'm doing alright with my kids, it still ain't right with Todd. I tried breaking it off a few times. I broke it off, changed my lock, and stayed with a friend for a few days.

He kept calling to find out when I'd be back home so we can talk. When I get back home, my house is spotless, candles lit, and dinner cooking. Smelling good. He greets me at the door to take my bags and help the kids in.

First thing I ask is how he got in. He said he broke a basement window and climbed through. I ask why. Told him, "I changed the locks because I didn't want you here anymore."

He says, "I know, that's why I broke the window."

So, I sat down and ate. I had to start praying. We were together for about six and a half years. Had some laughs in there but the bad has outweighed the good.

When he finally did leave, he took some of our things with him. I found that out after he left. But he was gone so I wasn't gonna bother calling for our things. Let it go.

189

I'm upset he took some things that can't be replaced, but he's gone, and I don't wanna entertain anymore of that mess.

He moved in with a friend. Thinking all the mess was behind us, I thought I'd have a night out with my cousin and ask him to watch his kids. He offered to watch all the kids at my place. Coo!

He calls while we're at the club wanting to know why I have condoms in my nightstand. I wanna know why he's going through my things.

He says he's taking them. That's fine! Call ends.
I'm having a good time with Latrice when he calls again and wants to know why I've been getting calls from a guy he knew in school.

I wanna know why he's going through my caller ID. Tells me I need to stop talking to other men, period and got upset when I told him I wasn't gonna stop anything for him and said he was taking our son and leaving. That's his son too so that's fine with me.

I cut the night short and went home. He was gone when I got there. Took our son and left the rest of the kids. I'm not calling him. I figure his son is fine with his dad for the night.

I call the next morning to tell him I'll be by after the boy's football games to get my son.

He says I can't have him back. He played that game before with On'yai. Held onto her trying to get me back. I'm not gonna worry about that right now.

I go on to watch both my sons play. The times were a little off and there was some distance between games. I caught the first half of one and the second half of the other.

I kept my word with Todd.

When I call to tell him, I'm pulling up to get my son he says his mom has him and doesn't answer the door when I knock. I walk around to the back of the building when he comes walking around the corner.

I head back to the front door while asking why his mom had him and when she's bringing him back. I get to the front of the building and there's my son standing at the screen door.

He starts crying for me when he sees me, so I reach for the door to let him out, but Todd pushes me back.

I tell him to stop playing with my son and reach again. Now his girl's standing at the door and locks the screen. The girl that he said was just a friend, like I care.

He pushes me again, so I ask his girl nicely if she can open the door and let my son out.

She asks Todd what he wants her to do.

Now I'm mad for real because both of them are playing with my damn son. "See, I wasn't even trying to go there with you but now you playin' with my son and I'ma beatcho ass."

Her, "Todd, you know how I get down."

Me, "Unlock the door and say that shit again."

He pushes me one more time and I black out. I snap out of it when I hear a voice I recognize yelling, "Mommy!" It's Jamal. He must've heard all the noise and got out the car to see what was going on.

When I snap out of it, I've got a metal folding chair in my hands over my head and Todd has his phone in his hand dialing. I already know he's calling the police, so I toss the chair at the door, grab Jamal and leave.

I pull around the block and park in the alley across the way so I can watch his place cause I'm going back for my son. I make a call myself and not to the police, but I have to call them off when I see the police pull up and I drive off.

Not going home, I go to Latrice's, just in case. Then I get a call from the police officer standing there with Todd.

He says to me, "Ma'am, you can't deny it, I'm standing here looking at him and I see the marks and blood."

Me, "I wasn't gonna deny it, I did it and how he gonna call the police on me when he got a warrant?" Officer said he hadn't run his name yet.

I say, "Well ya need to."

The officer, "Ma'am I'm trying to work with you, but you keep yelling at me." He really was trying to be nice.

Me, "Hell yeah, 'cause I'm pissed".

Now he's arrested Todd but won't let me back on the property to get my son 'cause Todd gave permission to leave my son with his girlfriend. The officer also says there'll be a warrant out for my arrest, and they can pick me up from my house whenever.

"Ah nah, you won't inconvenience me and my kids. When I get a babysitter, I'll come see you."

So, he said he'd wait a few days to put the warrant in. He really was trying to work with me, and I appreciate it.

Since I'm not allowed back on the property, I call Todd's mom to get my son for me.

She doesn't want to get involved and I understand that, but I need my son and she understands that, so she gets him for me.

Todd had put a wedge between his mom and I from the beginning, so we didn't always get along. He would tell me she was trying to take my son from me, so I'd be mad at her.

After this went down, she called, and we talked about it. She wanted to know why she couldn't have a relationship with her grandkids. I explained to her that Todd had me thinking she was trying to take my son.

She cried because she couldn't believe the lies. I got no problem with her being a grandma just as I had no problem with Todd being a father, but my kids are not pawns in some game. I won't let you play with my kids and I won't drag them through court. It don't take all that. Put the kids wellbeing first. We can all have a relationship with them, including the girlfriend. Damn!

We got over the lies and she's able to get her grandkids whenever she wants. If we could have communicated sooner, she wouldn't have missed out on the time she did miss with them and this was the start of a great relationship between us.

We were there for each other because she was raising her other grandkids and I was giving her breaks from them.

I kept my word and called a bondsman who told me I could do a walk-through. Went to do that and the clerk said she couldn't find a warrant for me. The officer kept his word and waited.

The clerk also told me I couldn't do a walk-through on my charge. I was gonna have to spend a night in jail. I don't know how she can see all that but no warrant.

No bond for me so I get a sitter and turn myself in a couple weeks later. Don't wanna take a chance on getting pulled over and taken, being put on the spot with my kids.

They said I have to be booked in by midnight for it to count as overnight so I go in about eleven pm. Get my orange jumpsuit. They have me freezing in that holding cell for hours. They know it does not take this long. I'm the only one in there. *Ya'll ain't that busy.* I need a dang blanket. They finally get me upstairs to a cell with a roommate for the night. Take the top bunk.

Then I have to pee, and I can't wait until checkout tomorrow. My cellmate is laying in her bed with her head at the end where the toilet is. Feels a little awkward.

I have to pull the whole suit down and I'm thinking she's gonna turn away when I squat.

Nope!

This old ass heffa is looking right *at* me. Like she ain't trying to miss nothin'.

Nasty ass!

Didn't even pretend to look away. Not even when I wipe my ass. I don't like jail. I'm looking at her while she's looking at me. I'm making sure she doesn't sit up while I'm squatting.

Next day we're moved for court to a cell with a few more folks. One of them asks for my socks.

No!

Her ass knew when she left home that day it was a good chance she was coming up in here. She knows the guards all too well.

They ask me what happened and one of them tells me I need to get rid of my baby daddy and get me a baby momma.

I just had one night. Man, I don't like jail. I plead guilty because I'm still mad and not trying to set another court date. Don't wanna look at him in court. *Yes, I did it and I'll do it again when It comes to my kids just like most would.*

Gave me two years of probation and anger management.

196

Had to meet with the anger management counselor to set up the classes. Thirty-two weeks. Every Tuesday and tells me I have to pay $35 every week.

You a damn lie. Nah! That ain't gon' work.
That's a whole other bill.
Nah!

Bad enough I have to take these damn classes thanks to my baby daddy, but then they turn around and tell me I have to pay to be in the classes every time I show up as if I wanna be here.

I told her, "I'm not paying you $35 a week like I wanna be here. That's too damn much." She told me my eyes are very intimidating and that I don't have to.

Tells me I can pay $10 and ask me not to tell anybody else in the class. That's fine and I won't tell.

Now I'm pissed off every Tuesday for the next thirty-two weeks. The counselor is asking about my childhood and I refuse to talk about that. She says I'm not participating, and my participation is a requirement of my probation.

"I'm not talking about my past in this class in front of everybody. I'll talk about the charge that landed me here and that's it. I'm not sharing all my business with these folks."

197

They're telling it all and breaking down. I'm not doing that.

Then the counselor asked the group to put themselves in DHS position and explain to one lady how we would have reacted in her situation when they took her kids from her.

So, it's my turn. I explained how it would've looked to me as DHS walking into a home with broken glass all over the floor, baby crawling around with bloody knees and parents on drugs fighting.

Dis bitch got loud with me. I didn't move. I remained calm and calmly shut her ass up.

Again, the counselor says my eyes are very intimidating and people are coming up to me after class telling me I scared them.

I wasn't trying to scare anybody. It's not like I got up and went for her. I reacted to dis bitch raising her voice at me and she apologized afterwards.

I told the counselor and my PO I don't have anger issues. He was using my son to get to me and his girl got on board with him. My son was crying for me while he's pushing me, and his girl stood next to my son with the door locked.

She didn't know why he was playing games with my son. Just going along with it.

I didn't tell her because I didn't want her to break up with him. I needed her to keep him occupied. I don't care about her thinking I want him. I'll take that. Small price to pay.

CHAPTER 17

Forgiving Mom

Back at work part-time and I'm ready to confront my mom on how she handled finding out what my dad did to me.

Her reaction still bothers me, and I don't want to speak to her about it because she's always on the defense. I get the feeling it won't go well. That she'll just yell at me and not address the issue at all.

I write her a letter instead. A few pages long. I wanna know why she smiled right after finding out. Why it was funny to her that someone hurt her daughter.

Letting her know how it affected me, I drop the letter in the mail. I'm anxious to read her response. I wait and wait and wait. Checking the mail every day to see no letter from mom.

After waiting for two months, I call her to see if she got my letter. I know she did. She says she did and hasn't responded 'cause she didn't know how. Didn't know what to say. Said she thought about it a lot while she was in prison and wanted to hurt him when she got out, but learned he died.

It wasn't enough but it was all I was gonna get from her. It doesn't comfort me, but I move on in my own way. My mom's not the apologetic type and I have to accept her at that. Life moves on.

My supervisor asks why I often wear baggy clothes. I like wearing Dickies cause they're comfortable and it plays into the shame I sometimes feel. I told her I don't like people looking at my body all the time and not all my clothes are baggy or mannish. I've even cut my hair a few times. Depends on the mood.

She compliments my cute shape and says I should be proud of my body. I try to change it up a little. Then she tells me I don't dress up enough on the days we're supposed to dress up. They always wanna push it.

So, I had to let her know that not all of us have a two-income home with one child.

201

Her and her husband are able to live comfortably working together with their one child. I don't have that life, so I let her know that if she would like to contribute to my clothing fund I will gladly dress up, otherwise I will continue to make sure my kids are taken care of and do what I can for me with what's left.

Naturally, I didn't get that clothing fund. I feel guilty shopping for myself if I'm not shopping for my kids at the same time and I can't usually afford them and me. I feel everything I have should go to my kids, but I listen.

She's not the only one to say something to me about my clothes. Before having kids, I was out shopping for myself every week with my mom's money. I'll work on treating myself.

I start shopping and new clothes are nice, but they don't heal. The wounds are still here. The clothes just help the cover up. The nightmares aren't as frequent but still come here and there. I continue to struggle with men and handling their advances.

It's not until I'm sitting in church one Sunday morning about seven years later that I truly forgive my mom, right before she gets out of prison from another stretch. I didn't tell her I forgave her, I told God. Just like when I forgave my dad.

I had her and my dad in mind that Sunday morning while the pastor spoke on forgiveness and decided it was time to forgive her and try to move on from that.

Are these forgiveness sermons just a coincidence?

She's released from prison shortly after. Myself and a few other family members wait for her at the bus station. She steps off the bus in a grey sweat suit, looking healthy and happy to be home.

Her hair is full and down a little past her shoulders. Her hair was always kept short before prison. We all get a hug and quick conversation with her in the short moment before she has to check into the halfway house. Not nearly enough time.

So much I'd like to talk about right now, but she's home and we'll have plenty of time later.

Time to see if we can build a better relationship.

CHAPTER 18

Momma Bear

I've always been very overprotective and strict on my kids as they were growing up, always keeping them close. My boys had a little more leeway than my girls. It's not fair, but unfortunately a lot of us parents are guilty of this one. They got to play outside more with friends without me hovering. The girls didn't really want to be outside that much anyway. They didn't enjoy the heat and dirt like that.

Even still I needed to know all their friends. I needed to know who the parents were. I questioned their friends on whether or not they were in school and what they did in their free time.

I randomly ask my kids if they were still virgins or doing drugs or alcohol and if they were trying to do any of those things. My boys laughed at me every time. I'd tell them they better get comfortable talking to me because I was the one that was gonna have to take them to the doctor if they little wheeny started burning.

I wouldn't allow my kids to date until they graduated. I feel like relationships are grown folk's problems and even grown folks struggle in that area, so kids shouldn't be worried about it. Plus, I figured a relationship would be a distraction from grades.

I tried keeping them involved in sports to help occupy their time. Too much free time can be an issue for some and I wanted my kids to enjoy their childhood as long as they could because not all kids get that choice. Some are stripped of their childhood for different reasons, so If you're blessed with maintaining your childhood, please enjoy it. Be a kid as long as you can.

My house has always been the spot for my kid's friends to hang out. I prefer it that way because I know my kids are safe and I love the sound of kids laughing and doing what kids are supposed to do. I also love seeing every race coming through feeling comforted within these walls.

I have a lot of patience since having kids. Not all parents want to be bothered with other folks' kids and that's alright. I try to keep my home as child friendly as possible so I don't have to fuss and worry about things getting broken. No fancy Knick knacks no glass tables to worry over fingerprints and broken glass.

Still, don't run through my house like it's a jungle gym and get snatched up. Have some manners.

I placed Jamal's clothes on his bed one day and when I walked out the room, I heard his company tell him he's lucky because his mom would never do that.

It was a simple gesture and the mom that doesn't bring her child's clothes to their room isn't wrong.

He could've gotten his own clothes from the laundry, but he was playing with his company and I didn't want to stop their game.

I may have overdone it in some areas but those are my kids and I made sure they always had clean clothes ready for the day, schedule planned out, something to eat and even a home baked dessert just because.

Once I got on my feet, there was always enough food to feed the drop-ins. There was also enough to allow me to help other single mothers. Allowing them to leave my home with grocery bags full of food and still plenty left in my kitchen for my home. Also being able to give away clothes, some with tags on them. I love to be able to share my blessings.

The kid's friends look forward to coming to my kitchen. I don't consider myself a chef, but it puts a smile on their faces, fills their belly's and I'm good with that.

When it came to their games I had to be there, from the PAL league all the way up to college.

At the end of practice in PAL league, my sons would ask if I saw that catch, that tackle or saw them get trucked. I loved the sound of the helmets cracking.

They knew where to look in the stands to find me at each game. I would be in the stands waiting for them to look up and nod at me and I would smile and nod at them. They knew if I was late to a game and they would be sure to tell me, "Mom, you were late."

I was there waiting for them to come out of the locker room so I could tell them good game or let them know it was gonna be alright when they cried.

I sat through the long softball games in the wind to support On'yai and cheer her on. The volleyball games she giggled through. She looked back and shhhhd me because you're not supposed to be loud at a tennis match, but that's my girl!

Watching ShyAnn wiz by me during her track meets. She was so proud and so was I.

Telling Raekwon to cut it out when his temper would flare up and he'd curse at the other teams and coaches in basketball.

Watching Sey'veon battle through wrestling, basketball, swimming, football, and jujitsu.

I've always been there for my kids. Never upholding them in their wrongdoing, but I'm here.

When the school called to tell me, Jamal was suspended for smoking weed I went up there and asked Jamal to tell me the truth. The principal and security said they smelled weed on his fingers.

Why they got their nose all on my son's fingers, I don't know, but Jamal said he smacked the weed from the kids hand when he handed it to him.

I took Jamal to the hospital for a drug test to make sure he wasn't lying to me. We got the results back in thirty minutes and I took him back up to that school and made them apologize to my son and lift that suspension.

The coaches would tell me that Jamal was the most respectful kid on the team. Every year he played I received compliments on his respectful behavior.

I was nervous when I got the call from the basketball coach that Raekwon was in a fight during practice. When he told me which student it was, I just knew my baby got beat up.

Aw Lord!

I was prepared to see my son bruised or bloody. He was waiting for me at the gym doors when I got there. We're looking at each other as I'm walking up to the gym doors then he smiles at me and I smile back. No blood or bruise.

My son!

"I guess you didn't get beat up!"

When we walk into the coaches' office, the big kid is sitting there with his face in a white towel catching the blood from his nose with his mom and little brother.

The coach I went to high school with was standing and waiting for me to come in so we can have this here meeting. I had Sey'veon with me. Sizing up the situation, if his momma wanted to get stupid, we had it.

The big kid started it by hitting Raekwon first. His mom said she didn't teach her kids to fight and that maybe she should call the police.

I told her maybe she should've taught him to fight if he's gonna be out here putting his hands-on folks and that she can call the police, but her son would be charged for striking first. That meeting ended very well.

The coach cried when giving his speech about Raekwon during the football banquet. It warmed my heart to know that I did that. Despite what I was raised in, I raised my kids in love.

Makes me feel good to see them leave such a positive impact on someone else just when I thought maybe I could've done something different, something better.

He's got a little funky temper, but yet and still he left a positive mark. The coaches loved him and even stayed by his side for an emergency appendectomy while I was away for the weekend.

They assured me they had him and would make sure he was taken care of, and they did. All the way to getting him home from the hospital. I love it when we as a community can pull together regardless of race.

The little things.

I became a massage therapist not just for the pay but for the flexibility it offered making it possible for me to be there for my kids as much as possible. This way I could be the one raising them and protecting without having to be concerned about childcare and who would be over my children.

I don't regret just making ends meet to be present for them. They didn't have all the latest, but I was there and they've loved having me around for their events and support at the school when needed. Also, for game and movie nights at home.

It all matters.

I love our relationships. Although I'm not happy about all that I went through, it made me the mother and woman I am today.

One thing I never could stand was somebody trying to tell me what to do with my kids when I'm the one doing this.

Nobody in my family helped me nor supported them but me and I'm okay with that 'cause I'm the one that had them but don't try to tell me what to do from the far sideline.

Don't stand here and judge my parenting. Look at your own home. I stood in the stands with my other kids watching the games. I made sure they showed each other love and support. Making sure they're here for each other so it warms my heart to hear them say, "I love you" to each other. I wasn't raised in that at all.

We laugh together, we cry together.

When I first moved back to Des Moines in 2010, they brought so many new friends home to our apartment. After we ate, I would put the leftovers on a tray and have my kids take it out to whoever needed it and they'd come back in with an empty tray.

Those kids were hungry and some of them were sleeping in the hallways, so I would let them sleep over until it began to affect my home in a negative way.

I learned of some of the troubles some of them were having at home and was able to speak to some of the parents. Didn't want to overstep my boundaries. I took a few of them out to eat so I could talk with them and encourage them. I couldn't do much because I don't have much myself, but I did what I could within my reach.

I fear for the youth without guidance.

In 2012, I kept having dreams of me and a little baby girl, so I knew I was gonna have a little girl, I just didn't know how because my tubes were tied after Sey'veon.

Then I got a call from my niece that she was having some trouble with DHS. They were trying to take her daughter, so I started going to court with her trying to help get her back.

Found out she was pregnant again while going through this. They wouldn't give us back the one they already had in custody, but I fought to get this one she was pregnant with.

They were mean to me at first. Put me in a box with everyone else.

After I got that assault charge from Todd, I was told I would never be able to work with kids or elderly, but they did the background check, I explained the charge and passed.

They started treating me better, with respect. I had just gone through this trying to become a registered in-home childcare provider and passed that too.

They ended up giving me the baby.

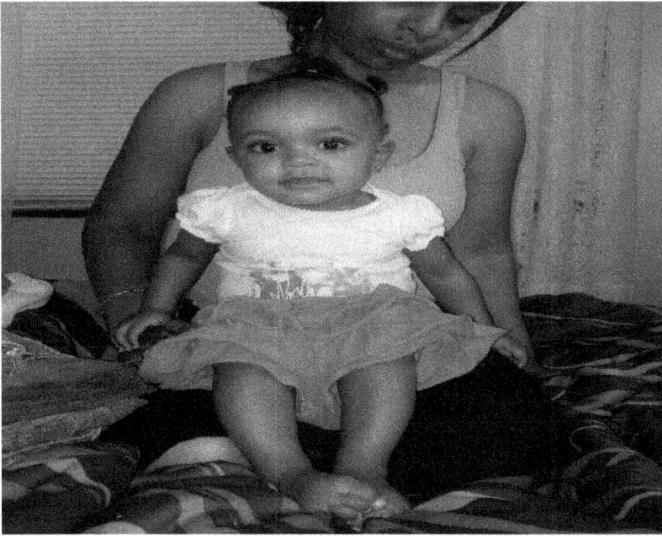

I didn't have much, but I felt blessed to be able to take her in and the kids were so excited to have a new sister. They couldn't wait for her to come home.

ShyAnn used money from her job to buy a few outfits for her new little sister. My kids, especially my sons, have her spoiled. She doesn't know she's adopted yet, but she will when I feel she can handle it and I keep communication open between her and birth mom, so she'll already have some connection to her.

With the older kids, I took ShyAnn, On'yai and a couple of my nieces out for lunch one day to talk about whatever they were going through.

Whatever they couldn't talk to anybody else about without the fear of feeling judged or shamed. They really opened up letting the little secrets out.

They cried. My nieces shared things they were ashamed of. ShyAnn even told me about her first kiss. She cried and made sure to tell me in public because she was scared I would come across the table and whoop her ass but that wasn't my reaction. She had just turned eighteen, so I wasn't mad at all.

This little talk went great for all of us and we discussed trying this once a month. On'yai went to school telling her friends about the lunch and they wanted to be in on the next one. The next time around more of them wanted in. Then I made my sons join in.

They said they wouldn't participate but they did, and they were laughing, having a good time. We did role play exercises. The next time some of their friends came and they had a good time. We did question and answer game and I cooked for them. Then On'yai and her friends wanted a movie night and so I did that at my home.

It was nice to hear high school kids screaming over a scary movie, mainly the boys. The sound of kids being kids.

The sound of innocence.

I'm always a mother first. I always think of what I went through and what these kids could be going through and it makes me want to help them. I want to help them hold on to their youth as long as they can.

On Mother's Day one year, On'yai gave me a framed pencil drawn eye with a few words underneath. I don't know where she got those words from but I love it. She didn't know what I had been through, but those words mean so much to me,

SHE LOVED SO MUCH, AND YOU COULD SEE IT IN HER EYES, WHERE SHE KEPT ALL THE HEARTS SHE PUT AHEAD OF HER OWN.

CHAPTER *19*

Manifestation of Pain

I fought in every relationship I was in except one and that was my marriage. It didn't last long at all.

I fought because the door to violence was open in my life. People talking crazy to me and hitting me first. With each relationship, I found myself becoming more and more violently aggressive.

My kids were asleep one night when one guy I was dealing with came in drunk and high, wrestled me down on the stairs and started choking me. The look in his eyes was like he was a completely different person.

I didn't have enough confidence in the strength of my hands to try and choke him back, but I knew to go for that adam's apple. When I got a hold of him there he jumped up in pain. Eyes wide open, looking at me like I'm crazy and he ran out the front door. He came back threatening my life a few times until I finally told him to go ahead and do it.

I had just gotten out of the shower, standing in the bathroom in just my towel and tired of his threats. "I'm right here right now, do it. Just don't touch my kids."

He stood there staring me into my eyes for a few minutes. I didn't budge, so he finally turned and walked away.

In another incident, he was standing over a frying pan one night with his back to me talking crazy, so I threw my empty glass hitting the cabinet over the stove.

Great aim!

Scared the shit out of him and glass shattered into the frying pan as he turned around with his eyes wide open. I stood there waiting for him to come at me, but instead he told me I was crazy, apologized, and cleaned it up.

When I was ready to end it, he wasn't going for it. I told him I was moving back home to Des Moines. I knew he wouldn't be able to leave the state so easy and I counted on that. He wanted to be able to at least drive me back home to see my hometown and hoping to get my new address though.

The only address he got was my sisters and the storage unit. He had to get back to Denver by bus. Once he returned to Denver, I told him it was over. Refused to give him my new address and stopped taking his calls. I received so many life-threatening voicemails, but it was over.

The next situation, at times, felt like an Ike and Tina Turner saga minus all the blood. He wanted his way and trying to shut him out wasn't easy. Things were fine until I was out with him one night and overheard someone congratulate him on his future baby.

It damn sure wasn't mine and he hadn't told me the news. When I got that news I wanted to end it. Apparently I was the side chick and couldn't tell because he spent so much time with me. Took me everywhere and answered all my calls.

I refused to let him in one night when he came banging on my side door. The side door was just outside my bedroom door where I was asleep in the nude. It was late and I did not feel like dealing with his mess, so I yelled out for him to go home.

That's when he threatened to go banging on my kid's bedroom windows to wake them up. I didn't want my kids involved so I hurried to the door before I could get dressed.

Soon as I cracked opened the door, he forced his way in and pushed me outside, locking me outside butt naked.

I was tired of him and his games. He wanted me to stand out there banging on my door, but instead of banging on the door like he wanted me to, I started walking alongside the house towards the street.

My younger sister Penny lived close by and I was walking in that direction.

He came running out the front door after me. By the time he reached me, I was already in the street. He grabbed me and pulled me back into the house where we fought and then had sex.

Still dealing with him, we went to a bar one night and I made a slick comment about him checking out a female that had just walked in the bar. I already knew he was dealing with other females and I was trying to get out of the situation.

He knew I was trying to pick a fight, so he took my drink thinking that would shut me up, but I wasn't drunk, that was my first drink of the night. I told him he could have it and I would just go get another one, so he followed me to the bar to tell the bartender not to make me another drink.

I know he didn't

I went back and forth with him and the bartender. He's facing me and puts his arm around my waist pushing away from the bar.

Quick thinking, I grabbed the fire extinguisher from the wall as I passed by it and the bartender came from behind the bar to help control the situation. While we were tussling, I swung the fire extinguisher at his head and missed.

The bartender and a couple others jumped in just in time. I missed his head and got his wrist instead as he put his hand up to block it. I wasn't letting go though. I wanted his head and they were all trying to get that thing out of my hands.

As we pass by Penny, she says to me, "Neesha, you're fuckin nuts!"

I smiled and said, "Yes, I am."

He wanted to put on a show in front of everybody and try to control me, so I participated. The next time I saw the bartender he told me I almost went to prison. He told me I was two inches away from killing that man. Had they not been right there to intervene, I would have.

It made me think, I didn't wanna leave my kids, so it was time for change. I had to get away from that one and the only way I could get out was to leave again. I packed up my house and kids to leave the state.

He showed up on moving day ready to fight some more, but I remained calm and ignored his pettiness. That irritated him to the point that he threatened me and spit in my face. I headed back to Denver.

I was tired of fighting and moving state to state to flee from these men. With my aggression growing, I had the thought that eventually the situation would end with one in the grave and one in prison.

I didn't want that, so once I got out of that last situation, I made sure not to get into another.

Men kept trying to talk me into relationships, but I couldn't. I was fighting to stay single because I was tired of fighting. I needed healing and I needed to be able to accept a different type of man. I need to see myself as worthy of a better type of man.

I had all types coming at me, but I was accepting the wrong ones. The toxic ones, but even if a good man had made his way into my life I may have ruined that, ran him off or ruined him because I was in too much pain. I stayed away for a little over a year.

Once I moved back home, I ended up with a friend from high school. We were going to church together and called ourselves trying to do it the right way which included giving up liquor.

I was trying to participate in the church functions when the Pastor asked me to but not all the women welcomed me. They treated me like I didn't belong and my assistance was not wanted. A couple of them got a little rude with me so I snapped back.

My kids asked me why I went off on one lady like I did, I didn't realize I did. She came at me though.

My ex-husband threatened to tell the Pastor on me for snapping on another. They don't get a pass just because they're in that building and calling themselves saved doesn't give them the right to act nasty towards others.

I wasn't all the way saved and clearly their judgmental asses weren't either. New to this and not turning the other cheek.

He kept trying to get me to be this sweet little thing he claimed to see in me, he didn't hit me, but I hit him. He got loud with me during a discussion about his baby momma. He was always on the defense of his actions.

She felt he was being disrespectful for having his future wife around their daughter when I was the one caring for the child while he was at work.

He was always defending his actions though and it was like once his voice reached a certain octane level before I knew it my hand took off and I couldn't catch it. I backhanded him and he jumped up calling me crazy, grabbed his jacket, and left.

That was before the wedding, I never hit him again, but the marriage still didn't last. I couldn't take all his drama and again, I did what someone else wanted me to do regardless of what I wanted and the fact that I wasn't happy with him in the first place.

I didn't want to be one of those who stayed and stayed miserable just because we said, "I do," so I quickly got out and have been trying to heal since. I don't want to settle again on what another HE wants.

I fought and prayed my way out of each of those situations. I've dealt with a man who knows the bible and knows it well, using scripture against me when he himself was a lie. Dealt with a man stealing money from my purse. Stealing money from my kid's piggy banks. Another slicing up my furniture with a knife. Breaking my kids PlayStation and Xbox consoles.

Then the thief came back stealing the PlayStation once I replaced it to go pawn it.

Stealing and pawning my camcorder with some of my kids' football videos still in the case. I was much more upset about losing the videos than the camcorder.

After my car accident I started doing Tae Bo at home to ease the physical pain rather than pain pills. While doing Tae Bo, I discovered that it also helped with the mental pain.

As I envisioned the faces of those who angered me with each punch and kick. I've enjoyed it so much that I'm still doing it seventeen years later.

Trying to find the space and time for my own healing was tough with my kids and everybody else relying on me for their needs.

I had to step away from the kids for a minute, so I went down by the bridge one day. Took a walk by myself just thinking, trying to clear my head. I stopped when I got to the middle of the bridge and stood there watching the water.

Rough waters.

I started feeling emotional and said, "God I need to know You're still here.

I need to know You're still with me and I'm not leaving this bridge until You show me, tell me, do something to let me know I'm not in this alone."

I was out on the bridge for a while waiting, fighting back tears. Then I noticed an older couple riding bikes over the bridge. The husband led the way and when the woman reached me, she stopped, taking one foot off the pedal.

She looked at me and said, "God said to tell you he still loves you and he's here!"

The tears fell immediately, and I asked her if I could hug her, she said yes.

I held onto her crying while she prayed for me. I left that bridge feeling better knowing He didn't check out on me.

Thank God!

CHAPTER 20

Reflections

My earliest memory is that of confusion and conflict.

My mom and dad fought over me and of course I didn't know why. My dad was always telling me how my younger sisters, by him, were jealous of me and didn't like me, and that may have been what put tension between us.

I'm really not sure how that tension developed, but it lasted.

I was always uncomfortable with them around. He would tell me how even his mom didn't care for me, but my grandfather did, yet he would take me to their house often and I felt out of place every time I went over there.

I Felt as if I didn't fit in with his side of the family, like an outcast.

All of their stares felt like judgement, my grandma, aunts, and uncles. Now I don't know if that's what it really was, but the things my dad put in my ear made me not care to be around them.

Being with my mom was more conflict. Always fighting with my sisters, my mom always yelling and beating us, and then her boyfriend doing the same.

Although once Anthony was gone, she didn't hit us nearly as much. I wasn't sure if she really wanted me or if she just didn't want my dad to have me. All the fuss to get me away from him, to bring me into a home of abuse and neglect.

At least that's what it looked like from my eyes. I always loved her but I didn't want to live with her. Sometimes it was good with her and sometimes it wasn't. The bad outweighed the good for me. I wanted to stay with my dad. I didn't feel the love of a nurturing mother. It was all about the hustle for her.

Being on our own so much and being locked away in the basement, put me and my sisters in survival mode. Sure there was plenty of food in the house. She fed us when she was home, but the hours she was away felt like too many hours alone.

Kids tend to act out in different ways from abuse and neglect, so that's where the stealing came in. It wasn't just because we were bad kids, it was a result of neglect.

When the opportunity came for me to stay with my dad, I was more than excited. I thought,

No more abuse and I can eat what I want when I want

At that time, it seemed like he was the only person in the world who was really there for me. I know my Aunt Jackie was there for us, but we didn't look at her as a save all. She had her husband and was creating her family with him.

My dad was the one who made me feel safe, special, loved, and spoiled. He made sure I didn't worry about my next meal. I was so spoiled that when I didn't want what him or his wife cooked, he gave me money to eat out. If my favorite outfit was ruined, he would take me to buy another.

He made sure I had what I wanted. He was the one always telling me how pretty I was, telling me how much he loved me and talking about all the money he would leave me when he died.

He made me feel I had him and only him in this world. My daddy was everything to me and my friends and family were jealous of the relationship I had with him.

He isolated me. He made sure to pit me against all my family.

When I moved in with him, he turned everyone in the house against me. He made sure that I didn't like any of them and they didn't like me.

He was always telling me how they were mad at me, didn't like me and didn't want me around, so of course I backed off from them. He didn't want me to feel like I had anybody in my corner but him and it worked.

With him isolating me, it worked out perfect for him to make his move. He knew I had no one to run to because all those relationships were ruined. He knew I had so much trust in him and loved him so much that I wouldn't go against him. He knew what he was setting me up for the whole time, and Daddy's little girl fell for it.

When he made his move, I had no one to go to. No one to ask, "Is God really okay with this?"

Deep down I didn't really think God was okay with it, but I couldn't go against my daddy. He already knew I was stuck, that's why he took my innocence with a smile on his face. I was so hurt when he didn't defend me in front of that doctor, but I had already been ruined so what's a little more pain and humiliation, right?!

Every year I get irritated around Valentine's Day.

Not a big fan of this day.

In all the years that I've been involved with someone it has never been about romance for me and I could not figure out why.

Not until the morning of February 11, 2021. Out of nowhere I realized that it was my dad who ruined this day for me.

At my age of 12, he came home from work with this big grin on his face and presented me this box right in front of his wife. This was before he began violating me.

Even though he ruined me, I kept that ring on my finger for years. Turning that ring on my finger several times a day every single day. Even though I was angry I wouldn't take it off.

Not until I had surgery in 2019.

After my surgery, I decided not to put it back on. I keep it in a Ziploc baggy along with the ring my mom gave me for my first Mother's Day.

Then another psychie comes to mind. Every November through December, around the time of his death and the loss of my child I begin feeling irritable and depressed; feelings that I can't explain to myself or anyone else.

These and the gun are reminders that he did not break me.

The photo on the cover is my senior high school photo taken while I was still living with my dad.

Still going through all that mess in that house. He had one of the shots from that shoot blown up and hung on the living room wall directly across from the front door.

Soon as you walk through the front door, you're greeted by this huge photo of me from the knees up. When you're sitting on the sofa facing the TV, you can also view my huge photo. As if he was somewhat obsessed with me.

I don't know if I would've made it in the modeling world or not, but I wanted to try. Thanks to his jealousy, I wasn't able to see that through.

I was so shy when other guys would approach me and didn't know how to interact with them. Liquor and my imagination helped the conversations along.
Lights, camera, action.

I wasn't schooled about proper positive relationships.

My mom never talked to me about boys, my body or sex, so all I had to go on was what my dad gave me. He had me and his wife against each other, so I couldn't talk to her either. By the time I got away from him I didn't even want to talk to anybody about those things.

It was too late because I had already gone numb, somewhat reckless and didn't know fear until faced with the moment of a man trying to have his way with me.

In that moment with a man, I became that little girl and just wanted to get away. Afraid of what could happen if I kept saying, "No."

I just wanted it over with.

I would drink and black out, trying not to think about it. I eventually became hypersexual. Programmed. In my relationships I was initiating sex often. Sex was all I could think about without even being horny and I never understood why until now. It just felt like something I should be doing.

For some, this is one of the outcomes of sexual abuse.

I would do it and almost immediately feel guilty and ashamed about it; sometimes even during the act, just to turn around and do it again.

I just felt that I had to keep doing it, getting nothing out of it and feeling bad about it. Running the streets, trying to outrun the pain, going through the motions.
When I asked my mom why she left my dad, she said he was crazy.

I've often wondered if that crazy could've told her what he was capable of doing to me. Maybe she could have tried harder to keep me from him.

231

On the other hand, if she had kept me from him to save me, I wouldn't have understood, and I would have been upset with her for keeping me from him. I wouldn't have known of that side of him, just that my daddy was the best, so I've never been upset with my mom for what he did. Just for her reaction when finding out what he did.

I think of the 'What if's' at times, but I don't dwell on them. I can't, because it happened, and I have to live with that.

Looking at other girls and wondering if they were just like me but afraid to ask. Wishing I had someone who was really for me. Not trusting who I could confide in or if it was worth telling.

Feeling like I was alone

I kept trying to run from the pain until I got pregnant. I didn't want kids, didn't want to be responsible for anybody else, but I wasn't about to get rid of my baby and thankfully my motherly instincts kicked in quickly.

Birth control failed me, but my kids saved me.

Having my children kept me from checking out completely. I wasn't trusting anybody else to take care of them or protect them. I had to make sure my kids never felt the pain I felt. I have a huge heart for kids because of my pain.

Because of my pain I see childhood as a blessing that too many are stripped of and I don't like to see that for any child.

I may not have been the best parent, but I've been the best I could be in my circumstances. Making sure they were better off than I was.

I finally reached a point of seeing the need to put more into loving myself and finding my voice. I've never been in love partly because I've never been with a man I really wanted to be with.

It felt routine.

Plus, I didn't like the mess I've seen others put up with because they said they were in love. All the cheating and abuse others stayed through for the sake of being in love.

I went along with the relationships I was in because they were so persistent about it, going on about how they needed me, and I'm tired of giving in to fulfill their needs and neglecting mine. Forcing myself to be there. In a constant battle in my head to make it work because he wants it and he's doing all this talking about how I make him feel.

Putting aside how he's making me feel. Because he says he needs me and loves me. Like being in that house with my dad over and over again.

I can't let another man manipulate me into a situation I really don't want to be in. A situation where I tell a man that I don't love him, and he tells me that I do.

I'm tired of my voice being irrelevant.

Can't do it anymore!

I've taken the time for myself. Not falling into relationships and even backing away from family in order to deal with me.

No more toxic relationships, friends, or family.

No more being around people who make it feel like it's always about competition.

Who's less than?
Tough man competitions.

For what?
What purpose does it really serve?

Trying to prove who's stronger or who can give off the better illusion of strength and perfection. One has to always be right and the other is always wrong.

Unhealthy!

How can you be for each other when you're always competing against each other?

We've all dealt with it in some form. I've dealt with that in relationships with men where it's him and his kids, and me and my kids. I voiced my dislike for it but it didn't matter. Whose kids get in more trouble, whose kids are better!

Same with family.

It's disgusting and I can't stand it! In a relationship, that's not being one, that's a home divided. It carries on and creates division amongst the kids. Now that toxicity has spilled onto the kids and they carry it on.

I want a relationship where we're on the same team, a family on the same team.

CHAPTER 21

Recycling the Abuse

The situations I shared in this book, I shared to show some of the damaging effects of trauma and untreated trauma.

The low self-esteem resulting from the condescending words of others. The constant abuse in all forms that leads you to believe you're not worthy of better even though you want better.

The abuse that lead me to recycle the abuse in other ways.

Sometimes my words towards men and even my kids cut like knives.

My drinking was my escape most of the time. In my drunken state I usually felt free and my aggression or anger towards men came out. I would playfully punch a man I knew in the jaw for just being next to me smiling and flirting with me.

Frustrated with men sexualizing me all the time. Maybe I would choke or backhand the familiar face next to me all while laughing just because.

I call it rough play not realizing I've really been acting out my anger towards my dad and all those other men that hurt me or any man that came flirting in a way I felt was disrespectful.

Subconsciously you continue down the same damaging path. You want off that path but can't seem to veer off. All these years living in damage. Continuing in this toxic behavior, laughing at my drunk self for hitting these men.

Feeling good about it because they shouldn't have been talking crazy to me. In reality they shouldn't have but my behavior has also been wrong.

No regrets

Lessons learned.

I'm grateful!

In my journey of healing I felt it was time to try therapy again. Time to let it out.

This time I did more research in trying to find a therapist who would fit me. My preference was a spiritual female therapist that wouldn't pull out a prescription pad.

I talked to a few by phone and email before finding one I felt a connection with. She gave me a survey in the first meeting and I scored a 9 out of 10 on the trauma scale. Surprising to me. I didn't want to talk about what I had been through, I just wanted her to fix me.

She told me that in the next visit she wanted me to tell her what happened to me. I looked at her like she was crazy.

"No, I'm not talking about that."

Told her that I had prayed, and God put this book on me, so I was going to need some help mentally and emotionally getting through the writing.

I wasn't trying to relive it with her, although I knew I would have to relive it to write this book and I knew it would be very emotional. I just wanted to be fixed.

Push your button and fix me please!

It was hard letting it out, but I did manage to get it out through the tears in the next visit. My first time giving that much information about it.

I joined a group called Kingdom Women's Group the year before and gave a small testimony. It brought a few of us to tears and led a few others to share similar stories that night.

Afterwards, the pastor walked up to me and said she couldn't wait to read my book, but the book wasn't in the plan at that point.

So, when I let it out to my therapist, I felt a slight release. I've been seeing her for months now and she tells me she didn't think she'd be able to help me in the beginning, but sees a big change in me now, a glow.

I feel better.

I won't say I'm completely healed, but I've made a huge step in the right direction. My smile is genuine now.

My mom cried when I told her I was writing this book. She was concerned about how it would make her look just like I was concerned about how it would make me look.

I've felt ashamed for so many years. I didn't hear from her for more than a week and when we did get back to each other she didn't want to hear about the book.

I get it.

She'd change the subject as soon as I brought it up. I wanted her to be open to talking about it because we both need this.

I need her to know I'm not okay.

As we started talking again, I continue mentioning the book and therapy trying to spark conversation and she slowly started asking questions and telling me how strong I appeared to be all these years and how she thought I was okay and over everything.

I let her know that I'm not and it's sparked more questions for understanding from her.

This is what I needed, what we needed.

I appeared strong because of so many leaning on me. I was never able to deal with my pain outside the locked bathroom because others needed me, especially my kids.

A friend once told me Denver made me mean. I didn't understand where that came from then, but now I do. The years I spent in Denver were dark and it makes sense because the pain and anger really set in after my dad died. Feeling like he was set free from suffering, but I had to stay and suffer.

I was pissed and snapping on everybody for everything. Those were very angry years. A lot of tears on my pillow from the nightmares.

The alarm clock I took from Denise after my dad died would go off without being set. My niece told me it was my dad trying to communicate with me.

I unplugged it and it's been unplugged since. Smelling him out of nowhere. Those were dark and painful years and I only had my kids. Although I poured some of my anger onto them, I poured all of my love onto them.

Mother's Day weekend this year, I struggled with this book. I couldn't stop breaking down. This was the first time I cried watching Medea's Big Happy Family when they talked about the girl being raped by her uncle and I've watched this movie plenty of times.

I couldn't write so I thought it would be a good time to let my kids read what I had so far. Maybe coming clean with them would help.

ShyAnn, On'yai, and Sey'veon read chapters 1-15. Sey'veon did as I suspected and read to a certain point and stopped. I knew he wouldn't read it all. When he finished, he walked up behind me as I stood looking out the front door and just stared at me.

No words and he still hasn't spoken on it, but it almost felt like an already close relationship just got even closer. I didn't wanna pressure him for his thoughts so I left him to process it. We can just sit together.

ShyAnn's first words as she cried were, "Now I understand. I understand why you raised us the way you did and I try to raise my son the same way. I get it now."

She reminded me of a night where she couldn't understand why I yelled at her for offering to take my boyfriend's plate up to him in bed when she was eleven. It was a reaction.

We also talked about me getting upset when Todd called down to her to bring him lotion when he got out the shower. I snapped on him for calling on her for that when he's sitting on the bed in just his towel.

On'yai cried and shared with me that older men make her uncomfortable even though nothing's happened to her.

It's understandable to me.

Jamal and Raekwon haven't read it yet. Jamal is worried it will ruin how he sees me and the rest of the family. He's very family-oriented. Raekwon thinks it's just about my financial struggles as a single mom. They've both agreed to read it when I'm finished.

Things have been better with my mom since she's been out of prison this last time. I never told her I forgave her for her reaction on what my dad did but we're better.

I'm sure my forgiveness was never a thought in her mind though. I'm sure she thought that moment was done and over with for me. Despite the hurt, our relationship has improved over these last eight years that my mom's been out of prison.

She found a job in management that she's held onto and is loving it. She's still a workaholic and now she can do that without worry for who's left at home. I enjoy visiting her at work and she loves to see her kids and grandkids pop up at her job. She does better with her grandkids than she did with her kids.

I still see a few of her old traits but she's much better still. I stop by her house to hang out. Even if it's just to watch a TV show we both like. I go over on some Sundays for Sunday dinner or she'll call just to see if I need to go to Walmart for anything.

We get our quality time in now because we want to spend time together.

She spoils my four-year-old grandson by ShyAnn. He's like the son she never had and he loves his great grandma.

As far as my feelings for my dad, well I still struggle.

It's a father that first teaches his daughter her worth.

What did I feel I was worth?

Not much!

I wasn't given a fair intro into the adult world as many of us aren't. Without a decent intro into the adult world, you tend to struggle with what's right, what's

243

wrong, and what's the norm. It makes it difficult to function properly.

The abuse can cycle from generation to generation, but you can make a choice not to inflict the pain you suffered onto the next generation, or anyone you come in contact with.

When you've been through trauma, you know it's a scar that doesn't disappear once the abuse stops.

You know that scar lives deep under the surface and takes years to heal or never heal at all without the proper care. You can attempt to break the cycle.

Although I always felt I was a good mom, it was because of him that I called my seven-year-old daughter a little floozy and yelled at her to, "sit your fast ass down," when she wanted to play tag with the boys.

I was mean to her, at times, because of him.

Seeing boys chase her, and her just a gigglin' like she was having fun, triggered me. I said those things to her because I didn't want her tempting those boys to do unwanted, or bad things to her. I didn't want them touching my daughter at all.

I didn't want her giving them any reason to think she liked them, or she wanted them to do things to her. I didn't want them forcing themselves on her and not stopping when she says, "No!"

I was scared for her and didn't know how to give her proper guidance at the time, or not to take my pain out on her. I just didn't want her having sex and seeing her playing with those boys scared me.

I didn't want her giving them any reason at all to go after her, so no I didn't even want my seven-year-old playing tag with boys. To me, that was acting inappropriate, "So sit the fuck down!!!"

I didn't just struggle with my kids, I struggled with men.

I'm just supposed to do what a man wants me to do sexually.

Being screwed for years by my dad, I felt ashamed of myself for years, but I don't feel that shame so much anymore.

I know now that it wasn't my fault. I was just being a child. For so long, I thought about torturing him every time he crossed my mind and If I could confront him now, I still don't know if I would be able to speak.

I would never want anyone to go through it in any way, though I know it's all too common. I hate that it's taken me so long to be able to get it out and truly begin to heal.

Unfortunately, I know I'm not alone in this and I would hope for a timelier healing for others.

I sometimes wonder what type of mother I would've been had I gotten it out sooner, or if I would've had kids at all had it not happened, but from my kids and word on the street, I've done alright.

I feel like my kids saved me. There are plenty of times I sit and wonder where I'd be if I didn't have them. When I think about it, I don't think I'd still be on this earth or I'd be strung out on drugs as some do from this.

Because of my protective instinct for my kids, I'm here.

I feel like God used them to save me and keep my heart from hardening.

Now my heart hurts for other kids. I feel for kids I see looking like struggle or hurt. On'yai keeps me connected with some, always bringing her friends home and having me feed them. She had me cater the girls basketball banquet and then the coach asked me to do it again the next year. I'm not a caterer, but I was happy to feed those kids.

When it comes to men I've struggled to orgasm because I'm not all the way there.

I try to be there when I'm with the man I'm in a relationship with, but it's hard sometimes. After while I'll tell him to just hurry up and finish. I can't focus on the moment with shame sometimes setting in, so I want him to hurry up and get it over with.

While going through therapy and the book I chose not to be with a man in any way. I didn't feel like I could do it while facing this.

I would like to get married to a man I actually want to be with and when I do I want to be all the way there with him and It starts with me.

As far as my relationship with God, well I didn't walk away. I strongly believe that He is the reason my heart did not harden. He is the reason my heart stayed pure through it all.

He is the reason I'm able to feel so much warmth and compassion for others. He is the reason for my good health, if ya know what I mean.

I do believe He drove me home all those drunken nights that I blacked out and woke up the next morning not remembering the drive home.

I wake up the next morning looking around my room and thanking God.

I go outside to look at my vehicle and thank God.

I know I've been a mess and yet I thank God for keeping me.

I still get frustrated at times but I don't lose faith. Instead I ask for forgiveness and guidance.

I KNOW THERE'S GREATER FOR ME AND I'M NOT GIVING INTO THE PAIN.

I know there are both men and women with stories worse than mine but please fight through it. Fight to heal not just for you but for those close to you. For your kids that need you. For your family that loves you. For your friends who are trying to be a friend to you, but they can't because you're hurt won't allow them to get too close.

Yes, it happened, but I'm still here.

Life is still moving forward and so am I.

For those trying to love you past your pain and those who need your strength and guidance.

Love and Forgiveness can bring Healing.

Healing can dissolve hate.

For those who tell me, "Your ass is crazy." This is why.

For those who tell me, "You have no filter." This is why.

For those tell me, "You're a beautiful person inside and out." This is why.

This is my path.

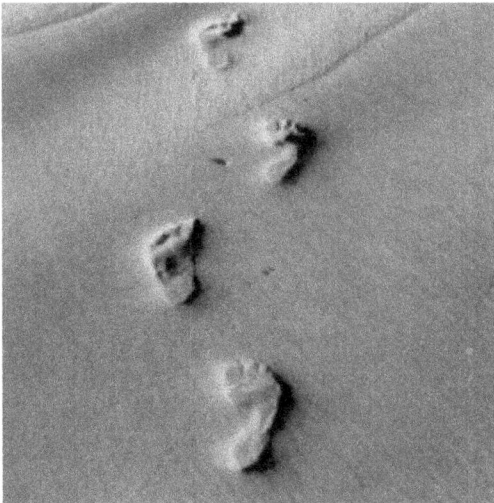

Never judge the person standing in front of you.

You don't know the path they took and nine times out of ten, you couldn't handle their path.

249

CHAPTER 22

Let's Heal

You're damaged or hurt and it's okay.

It's okay because it's not your fault and you don't have to stay there, but you do have to admit it so you can change it.

Accepting who you are right now isn't saying this is who I am and that's that. You're admitting to yourself that something bad happened to you and you're not okay.

You need help and it's okay to say I need help. That's strength.

Say it and seek it

Don't remain in that unhealthy state.

You can change it.

You don't have to check out on yourself. That's not the answer to the problem.

You can solve the problem by getting help. Let it out even if that means seeking professional help. Find a therapist that fits you.

I don't believe that any therapist with a license is the right fit for all. I tried that. You have to find the one that's right for you. It's a relationship. You have to vibe. Feel comfortable with that therapist. That therapist has to work for you and your needs.

I needed one that didn't just see me as a paycheck. One that wasn't anxious to throw drugs at the problem as soon as you walk through the door, though some may need that for balance.

I didn't want to mask my problem, I wanted to face it head on knowing all those emotions would come back. That's what I needed in order to find my healing. I want to encourage you to find the positive healing that fits you.

Forgiving my dad was hard.

Him telling me that God said if I forgave him, He would ease his pain was tough. Those words came off selfish from him. I was confused about his relationship with God or how they could even have a relationship at this point.

I definitely didn't want to hear it.

The pain and those words were eating me up, so I decided to go ahead and forgive. I didn't do it for him, I did it for me. I thought it could help me. Although his death brought me more pain initially, I still stand by forgiveness.

Some questions that may be going through your mind as you read my book may be:

Question: Could I stand in his face and forgive him?
Answer: I honestly don't know.

Question: Do I still think of hurting him?
Answer: Yes, I do.

I don't regret telling God that I forgive him though. Looking back on my relationships now, I realize I was in a comfort zone.

I grew up in toxic homes and continued on the path in my relationships. I stuck with what I knew. Time for change. It took a long time, but my healing has begun and I'm happy. I feel the difference. I see the difference in the effect I have on others.

Although I'm sure it will be a continued process, I'm happy to be on my healing journey.

On another note, it happens all too often where a child tells her mom that mom's boyfriend sexually abused her or attempted to, and the mom immediately gets upset with her daughter and finds fault in her child instead of the boyfriend.

She becomes overwhelmed with jealousy and wonders what he sees in her daughter that he doesn't see in her. She's asking herself that question in the wrong way.

To that woman, that mother; I say to you, "You need to address him and not her. That child is just being a child and if she's behaving in an adult manner then that's something you need to look into further and you still address that grown ass man for taking an interest in your child."

"You do not continue in a relationship with that man who wants to have sex with your child. When you do, you are just as much the problem as he is. You need to be dealt with as well. You are a part of the damage done to that child. You are responsible as well."

"You don't get jealous over no child. You have insecurities that you need to deal with. Don't allow your child to suffer because of your insecurities. Don't put your child out of the house or let him and her both stay while he continues to abuse her. You are the problem as well!"

Let's find the time and space to heal.

Because of the 2020 pandemic and quarantine, I was able to deal with all the anger and pain at home without having to cover my scars so others wouldn't stare.

Very convenient for me.

I know that not everyone is able to isolate and shed these scabs behind closed doors and that's okay.

Know that you are not alone and should feel no shame.

YOU ARE LOVED AND HEALING IS POSSIBLE

www.ingramcontent.com/pod-product-compliance
Lightning Source LLC
Chambersburg PA
CBHW060301100426
42742CB00011B/1826